D0588739

awesome
on the inside

how to be changed by God
from the inside out!

tim hawkins

Awesome on the Inside © 2005 Tim Hawkins

Published in Australia by Hawkins Ministry Resources
42 York Road, Kellyville, NSW2155, Australia
Phone: (+61 2) 9629 6569
Fax: (+61 2) 9629 6569
E-mail: info@hawkinsministry.com
Website: www.hawkinsministry.com

This edition published in the UK by The Good Book Company Ltd
Elm House, 37 Elm Road, New Malden, Surrey KT3 3HB, UK.
Phone: 0845 225 0880
Fax: 0845 225 0990
E-mail: admin@thegoodbook.co.uk
Website: www.thegoodbook.co.uk

ISBN: 978-0958184311

Printed in the UK by Bookmarque

Contents

a heart that is powerful

section 1

"This book really helped me to get a better understanding of what Jesus has done for me. It's really helping me to put God first! Once I read the first chapter, I was really looking forward to the rest." **Lisa, Year 10**

1 the problem of just "looking good"

Image is everything

There's something incredibly unfair about being a teenager.

> With all the hassles you face...
> With all the pressures you put up with...
> With all the so-called friends who will let you down...
> With all those times with your parents when they don't seem
>   to understand anything that's going on for you...

Right in the middle of the most humungous time of growth and change that you've ever experienced since the moment you were born comes **this** pressure...

> *"You've gotta look good!"*

Somehow in the middle of struggling with your difficult feelings that are deep down on the inside, you now have to look "good" on the outside as well. Despite what the TV ad says – image **is** everything!

You know the pressure. Your friends all have designer label jeans. But you're wearing jeans that your mum bought from the bargain bin at Tesco! You can hear the judgemental tone in your friends' voices as they ask that catty question *"Where **did** you get those things?"*

It's the night of the big party. You're spending hours getting ready for this special event. As you check yourself in the mirror, you notice something that has the potential to turn your "night of nights" into an embarrassing social disaster. There it is – right in the middle of your chin. Yesiree – we're talking about the dreaded enemy of puberty – **you've got a zit!** A big, red, hairy, throbbing, pussy zit! You apply every bit of chemical warfare known to humankind to eradicate this monster – but there it stands – tall and proud – ready to erupt like Mt. Vesuvius. You might be the greatest teenager in the world, but you know that when you meet people at the big party that night, all they will see in you is a helpless victim suffering the ravages of terminal acne.

Or maybe you've decided to ditch the cool image. No longer are you going to be pushed around by the fashion labels. No more will you be a victim of the glossy magazines. You're gonna look different. But you've gotta take care to make sure you get that "different" look just right. You've gotta choose whether you get your clothes from the Army Surplus Store – or from the charity shop. You spend hours getting your hair just right so it looks like you haven't touched it. You gotta make sure your jeans are ripped in all the right places.

It can be hard work getting that "different" look just right.

> *"Hang on – I*
> *don't even care what I*
> *look like!"*

Yeah – I know. You roll out of bed and put on the same clothes you wore yesterday. Your idea of changing your underwear is to turn them inside out. You wear a hat 24/7 cos you can't be bothered brushing your hair. You refuse to submit to our society's obsession with cleanliness – and you only shower when your mum forces you to. But can you see – **that's** your "look"! **That's** the image you want to portray to everyone. So whether you're cool or grungy – you know that your image – the way you look – still matters to you.

What everybody notices

And the reason that your image matters to you? **Because it matters to everyone else!**

> There are some guys hanging around after school. They notice a bunch of girls walking up the street. They start to talk to each other and make comments about the quality of the femininity that is fast approaching them.

So what are they talking about? Some of these girls might have the friendliest personalities in the known universe. Some of them have outstanding intellects that will guide them towards becoming the top neurosurgeons and nuclear physicists of this century. Others have a deep faith in God, which makes them some of the most supportive and faithful people you could ever imagine.

What are the guys noticing? What are they talking about? What are they focussing on? They're talking about **what the girls look like!** Image matters to other people.

They tell me that girls are very similar. Guys can have all sorts of admirable qualities on the inside – all sorts of potential for the future – these guys could well be developing as the leaders, the achievers, the poets, the dreamers, the dads, the lovers, the inspirers of the emerging generation.

What do the girls notice?

"Cute backside!"

POWERFUL Maybe you realise that this is incredibly shallow and demeaning, but deep down, you know that what you look like really matters to others.

That's why every girls' magazine features yet another miracle diet that will give you the body you've always dreamed of. That's why every guys' magazine will show you ways to increase your muscle tone and develop your abs so you can show off your perfect six-pack. How you perform at sport, or music, or dancing, or school, or whatever – you know it matters to other people and you know it matters to you.

The big companies of the world make squillions because they know we will spend up big to make our image look right. We will buy hair gel, skin cream, deodorant, expensive shoes, brand-name fashion, accessories, makeup, sound systems, cars, sunglasses, mobile phones... in fact we will buy **anything** that makes us look the way we really want.

Your Christian "image"

There's even a Christian version of "looking good on the outside". And I don't just mean wearing the latest WWJD wristband, buying a new snazzy cover for your Bible, or spending your money on any of the items in the vast array of Christian merchandising like T-shirts, jewellery, perfume, bookmarks, bumper stickers, backpacks etc. And I'm also not just referring to adding to your already overflowing collection of Christian CD's because "there's another praise and worship album out – and I simply **have** to buy it!"

"You want people to be impressed with you – don't you?"

Here's what I mean. Sometimes it's easy to look good as a Christian "on the outside". You know – smile and be polite to people, show up at church, read your Bible, say your prayers, don't break any

obvious commandments, get involved in your church youth group, raise your hands and look passionate in every worship song, always go forward at the appeal at the end of the talk and show everyone else what a great, humble and repentant person you really are.

While all of these things can be real and genuine, there can be the subtle temptation to do things that look good on the outside. I mean, you want people to be impressed with you – don't you?

God wants to change you from the inside!

But there's an emptiness to all this. You know that if you simply put on a brave face on the outside, but inside it feels like you're still failing, you know how fake that feels. When everyone else judges you by what you **look** like, rather than by what you're **really** like, you know how hurtful that can be. You can buy any number of books that will teach you how to act well "on the outside" – so that you impress people and succeed in the world.

But you know that unless that change is deep and powerful – and comes right from the centre of your being – no amount of spiritual plastic surgery is going to change the way you really feel. God is not fooled by simply changing the outside. People who get to know you are not fooled by it either. And you know what – **you** know how awful it feels when you are pretending on the outside, when deep down you know you are still hurting.

Three principles that will change your life

Here's the good news: God wants to change you from the inside! God has already made you to be an awesome person, and he wants to keep changing and growing you! And he's not just interested in getting the "outside" right. He wants to bring a change deep within you – so that **all** of you will grow to be the fantastic person that he has destined you to be.

In this crazy world where young people are being torn inside-out to live up to what everyone else expects of them, I want to introduce you to three Biblical principles that can make sense of the whole shemozzle. Three foundational truths that can help you make sense of your life. Three guidelines from God himself that will help you to become the man or woman that he has destined you to be. Three truths that will help you to become "awesome on the inside".

Ready?

Take a deep breath... here they are...

1. **Your inside is more important than your outside.**
2. **To change your outside, work on your inside.**
3. **What's on the inside will always come out.**

Heh? Confused already? Come on, you can do this! Check back over the principles again – line by line – and I think you will see that they make sense. Let's have a look at them one by one.

2 the inside is more important

Principle 1
What's on the inside is more important than what's on the outside.

This first principle is true of everything in the universe. Everything? Yep – everything! The way things look on the outside does matter, **but what it's like on the inside is far more important!**

It's true for cars

My son Josh had reached the stage of his life where he wanted his own car. He had left school – he was driving – he was earning an income. He really wanted a second-hand VW Golf. He came to me one day and said *"Dad – I've found the car I want!"*

> *"Great"* I replied. *"Let's go take a look at it. Where is it?"*
>
> *"It's on the internet!"*
>
> *"The internet????"*

He'd found the car of his dreams on one of those on-line auction sites where you place your bid to win the auction.

> *"Josh,"* I said, with that typical fatherly concern in my voice.
> *"You can't buy a car off the internet!"*
>
> *"Why not?"*
>
> *"Josh – you've got to check it out. You've got to go and see it!"*

"Dad – I know exactly what it looks like. There are four photos right here on the website!"

We rang the guy – we went and looked at the car – it looked okay on the outside – I mean... it was red... (and we all know that red cars go faster!) – so Josh bid for the Golf, and secured the car of his dreams for £500.

I told Josh that I would pay to have our mechanic give it a service – fix anything that needed it – and make sure it was okay on the inside. I should have guessed that something was wrong when my mechanic rang me at the end of the day, and asked if he could keep the car for a few more days. Then, after those few days had passed, I got the bad news from my mechanic.

"You can't afford to keep paying me to fix this car. But as a favour to you, if I can keep it for a few weeks, we'll work on it 'in-between-jobs' and just charge you for the parts."

3 weeks and **another** £500 later, Josh's car had been fixed on the inside. We had learnt a valuable lesson:

"What's on the inside is more important than what's on the outside".

It's true of everything

That principle always holds true. **What something is like on the inside is always more important than what it looks like on the outside!**

You can have the snazziest looking computer ever invented, but if it's corrupted by a virus on the inside, it's useless.

You can have the sleekest and sexiest mobile phone on the market – but if you've just dropped it in the toilet so that it's wet and decaying on the inside, it's worthless.

You can have a great looking boyfriend or girlfriend, but if deep down below the surface, you don't trust each other – and you know that they're cheating on you – it doesn't matter how great they look, you know that your relationship is history. What's on the inside is more important than what's on the outside.

It's true as a Christian

Jesus taught this same principle to the religious leaders of his day. We're gonna look at Matthew 23, where Jesus is talking to a bunch of people called the "Pharisees". They were

> ## "What's on the inside is more important than what's on the outside"

the religious leaders of the day. As far as anyone was concerned, you couldn't get anyone who was more godly than the Pharisees. These were the "good guys" in the following-God department. They all read their Bibles. They all said their prayers. They gave money to the poor. They went to church – every week without fail. They would have gone to their Bible study group, attended leadership training, played in the band, done car-park duty, trained for evangelism – they did everything that you would expect someone who was absolutely committed to following God to do.

They had a reputation among the people for being the holiest, the purest, the most passionate, the most prayerful. These were the guys you would look to if you were struggling in your own faith and you wanted to be inspired to become the person that God had designed you to be. They ran big and active churches – probably wrote best-selling books on 7 keys to getting right with God. You could buy their CD sets and listen to them in your chariot as you drove home.

Their reputation for following God was fantastic. They looked absolutely "perfect" on the outside. Listen to what Jesus says to them:

Matthew 23:27-28

"Woe to you, teachers of the law and Pharisees, you hypocrites! You are like whitewashed tombs, which look beautiful on the outside but on the inside are full of dead men's bones and everything unclean. In the same way, on the outside you appear to people as righteous but on the inside you are full of hypocrisy and wickedness."

Ouch! Jesus is teaching them Principle 1 – *What's on the inside is more important than what's on the outside*. He calls them "whitewashed tombs". Can you imagine the scene in a cemetery – where there's hundreds of tombs where bodies are buried? Can you picture that some of these tombs are beautifully kept? Gleaming white marble – hand-carved headstones – perfectly-mown lawn with an assortment of pretty flowers – everything clean and sparkling – "white-washed" on the outside.

Jesus says to these religious leaders "You look that good on the outside. But inside – you are like rotting corpses – decaying flesh – maggot-ridden manure."

Ever feel a bit like that? You look great as a Christian on the outside, but you're falling to pieces on the inside?

Jesus is teaching us a very important principle. ***What's on the inside is more important than what's on the outside.***

Christianity is never about the outside only

Somewhere along the line, we've lost the plot about what it really means to be Christian. It's like there are 2 lists. One list is all the good things you can do – the other list is all the bad things you can't do. (You can call them sins, if you like). We've sort of worked out that a Christian is a person who does all the good things on List A, and doesn't do any of the bad things on List B. We've somehow been tricked into thinking that it's only your **behaviour** that matters as a Christian. If you can get to the end of the day, and tick off each bad sin on List B and say *"I'm not doing that"*, that somehow that's what it means to be alive in Christ.

But that's crazy! You can't define a Christian by what they **don't** do!

I heard of a community once that was virtually perfect in not disobeying the commandments. No-one had hurt anyone else. No-one had got drunk. No-one had been sexually fooling around with someone they weren't married to. In the previous 12 months, no-one had uttered one swear word. No one had told one lie.

Some people would say: *"This is the perfect example of a Christian community. No-one sins!"*

I'll tell you why no-one sinned. It was a cemetery. It was a community of dead bodies. They were incapable of sinning. Perfect obedience on the outside. But on the inside, they were rotten decaying corpses.

> **"Christianity is never about the outside only"**

Jesus is not just trying to change you on the outside. If you say your prayers, and read your Bible, and you're nice to everyone, and you can say from memory the Lord's Prayer, and the Apostles Creed and the 10 commandments... if you attend a nice Christian school and put a nice uniform on you so you look fantastic on the outside... if you could learn good manners so you are polite, and pleasant, and co-operative... everybody in the world might love you (especially your parents!)...

But maybe on the inside you might still be a rotten and decaying spiritual corpse. Maybe on the inside you would resent having to be so "perfect" for everyone. Maybe on your inside you would be just longing for the day when you no longer have to live up to everyone else's expectations.

Ever felt like that? Then hopefully you have now learnt Principle 1 – *What's on the inside is more important than what's on the outside.*

3 all change starts from the inside

Principle 2
To change your outside, work on your inside.

Or – to put it another way – "Growing your **character** is more important than growing your **reputation**."

Let me explain what I mean by that.

Your **reputation** is what other people **think** you're like.
Your **character** is what you're **really** like.

Your reputation is what is seen on the **outside**.
Your character is what is real on the **inside**.

Your reputation

Your reputation is what other people think about you. Your reputation is one of your most valued possessions. If you lose your reputation – then you have lost something incredibly valuable.

When I was at school, there were lots of kids who had all sorts of reputations:

> Barry had a reputation for being a cry-baby.
> Erica had a reputation for being teacher's pet.
> Glen had a reputation for getting lots of girls into bed.
> Joanne had a reputation for being into the drug scene.

You can probably think of lots of people that you know, and you can think of lots of reputations that they have. Are these reputations true? Or are they mere gossip? (Good question – more about this later!)

You see, reputations can be accurate, or they can be entirely inaccurate.

Have you ever heard of a businessman who had a reputation for being successful and rich, but it was later found out that he was on the verge of bankruptcy – and had conned a lot of people out of their money?

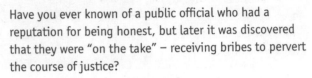

Have you ever known of a public official who had a reputation for being honest, but later it was discovered that they were "on the take" – receiving bribes to pervert the course of justice?

Have you ever heard of a youth leader – or a children's worker – who had the reputation of "caring for children" – but later it was discovered that they were using those same children for their own pleasure?

Reputations are not always accurate!

Do you know what your reputation is? What do parents and teachers think of you? What do your fellow-students think of you? Is your reputation accurate? Or do people believe things about you that you know are simply not true?

Sometimes growing up can be cruel. You can be called all sorts of names. You can be picked on in all sorts of ways. You can even be teased and bullied. You might have a reputation that you know you don't deserve.

Maybe someone has spread stories about you. Maybe someone made up a nick-name for you one day – and the name kinda stuck – and deep down you hate it. Maybe there are some who simply pick on you – and everyone else just seems to join in.

> **"Your reputation is what other people think you're like"**

You see, your reputation might not be accurate. You might have a **good** reputation that you don't really deserve, or you might have a **bad** reputation that you don't really deserve. Here's the good news – you **can** do something about it! Let me now introduce you to something that is far more important than your reputation.

Your character

Your character is what you are really like on the inside **whether anyone knows about it or not.** Other people can change your reputation, **but no-one else can change your character.** If you have a good character – a Christ-like character –an honest character – **then no-one can ever take that away from you.**

Remember, your **reputation** is what other people **think** you're like. Your **character** is what you're **really** like. Your reputation is what is seen on the **outside.** Your character is what is real on the **inside.**

> **"Your character is what you're really like"**

You cannot control your reputation. **But you absolutely can control your character.** You can make the decisions now that will strengthen and grow your character so that you become the person that God wants you to be.

Now – here's the great news – **If you want to change your reputation – work on your character!** Because eventually, your character will show through.

This is Principle 2. ***"To change your outside, work on your inside."*** Or to put it another way, *"To change your **reputation**, work on your character."*

What Jesus teaches

Look at how Jesus teaches Principle 2 to the religious leaders of the day.

> *Matthew 23:25-26*
> *"Woe to you, teachers of the law and Pharisees, you hypocrites! You clean the outside of the cup and dish, but inside they are full of greed and self-indulgence. Blind Pharisee! First clean the inside of the cup and dish, and then the outside also will be clean."*

Jesus describes the "fake" nature of these religious leaders. He says that they spend their time *"cleaning the outside of the cup and dish, but inside they are full of greed and self-indulgence."*

Here's the deal. Jesus says that these leaders focussed far too much on looking good on the outside – they cared too much about their reputation – and never bothered fixing what they were like on the inside. Their **reputation** was strong, but their **character** was weak.

Now, what advice did Jesus give to people who were looking good on the outside, but never bothering with the inside?

> **Matthew 23:26**
> *"First clean the inside of the cup and dish, and then the outside also will be clean."*

Here is Jesus teaching Principle 2 ***"To change your outside, work on your inside."*** Jesus instructs these Pharisees to clean up their character on the inside – and then (and only then) will their outside (their reputation) also be really clean.

That means that you can do the same thing. If you want to have a genuinely good reputation, **work on your character** to bring it into line with what God wants. Because as you work on your character, your **reputation will change!**

If you're reputation isn't what it should be, start the change from the inside out. Start working on your character. Allow God to change your heart on the inside, and you will see fantastic and awesome changes happen on the outside.

How do I change on the inside? How do I grow and develop my character? How do I become truly "awesome on the inside"? That's what the rest of this book is about!

But first – one more principle we need to learn.

4 the inside always comes out

Principle 3
What's on the inside will always come out

Okay – let's just recap the Biblical principles we have looked at:

> **Principle 1. What's on the inside is more important than what's on the outside.**
> **Principle 2. To change your outside, work on your inside.**

Let's now add the last Biblical principle that can set you on the right track as you grow and develop as God's child:

> **Principle 3. What's on the inside will always come out.**

It's true in your own life

In our day-to-day life, we can be involved in all sorts of "cover-ups". All sorts of situations where we're pretending on the outside, yet never dealing with the real issues on the inside. But as sure as night follows day, you need to understand Principle 3 – *What's on the inside will always come out*.

Your guy shows up for the big date, and he looks good and he smells good. He's sprayed on 2 litres of *Hugo Boss for Men*. And finished off with a few layers of *Eau Savage*.

> ## "What's on the inside will always come out"

On the outside, he smells good. Real good. But later, after your big date at the "All you can eat pig-out night" at the chinese restaurant, as you

snuggle up to each other, accompanied by sweet romantic music, you realise that while he started off smelling real good on the outside, you discover to your horror that underneath it all –
he stinks! I mean, he really stinks!

In front of your very eyes (and more importantly, in front of your very nostrils) he demonstrates the truth of Principle 3 *"What's on the inside will always come out."*

> *What's on the outside can make a great first impression...*
> *But it's what's on the inside that really lasts.*
> *Eventually, what's on the inside will always come out.*

The same is true about your character and your reputation. You can "cover up" on the outside for a while, but eventually, what's on the inside (your character) will show through. No matter how clever you are, at some stage you'll be caught out.

It's true in everyday life

Think back to some stories where someone famous suddenly had to drop out of circulation. Maybe it was a famous rock-star who was arrested for doing the wrong thing. Maybe it was a famous sporting star who was exposed in their private life. Perhaps it was a well-known politician or business leader who suddenly found themselves being pursued by an investigative journalist.

"You don't want people to think you're not doing well as a Christian!"

What caused these famous people to suddenly be brought into disgrace? What stopped their careers and brought them into disgrace? What took them off the dizzy rise to the top and threw them on the scrap-heap of failure? What took them from being a hero to being a zero?

It wasn't normally because they made a mistake with their job. It wasn't usually because they were found to be incompetent. People don't usually fall from grace because they didn't have enough talent in their chosen profession. People don't usually "blow it all" because they hadn't sharpened their skills enough. Very rarely is their failure due to something on the outside.

Usually, it's their character that lets them down. There is usually something fundamentally wrong with who they are on the inside. There are issues in their private life that they have never dealt with. And one day, sooner or later, Principle 3 always comes true – *"What's on the inside will always come out."*

It's true being a Christian

It's exactly the same with being a Christian. Principle 3 always applies.

> *What's on the outside can make a great first impression...*
> *But it's what's on the inside that really lasts.*
> *Eventually, what's on the inside will always come out.*

You know how it goes. You go to church... or you go to your youth group... or you go away on a Christian camp and you're surrounded by stacks of people who are all Christian. It's great to be a Christian and it's cool to be a Christian. And you certainly don't want people to think that maybe you're not doing well as a Christian.

Cos you don't want them asking questions. And you don't want them challenging you. And so – you pretend. You make sure everything looks okay on the outside.

> *"Sure – I had a great time with God this morning.*
> *I'm really getting stuck into his word.*
> *I'm seeing some great answers to prayer.*
> *And yes, I'm obeying him just fine.*
> *Hallelujah! Praise the Lord!"*

On the outside you can look just fine. But maybe on the inside, it's all collapsing.

> *Perhaps you haven't looked at your Bible this year...*
> *Or maybe you're doing everything in your own strength and not asking God for help with anything...*
> *Possibly you're sexually fooling around with someone, but pretending it's okay...*
> *Perhaps when you're away from the Christian group, you speak to others in a way that's hurtful...*
> *Or maybe it's just what you think about day in day out that you know doesn't give honour to Jesus...*
> *Or it could even be that right now, you're not even sure that you want to keep following Jesus – and you might just be on the point of giving up on him... and maybe reading this book is your last shot at hanging in with him?*

For some of you, there is a real struggle going on inside. And for some of you, the struggle on the inside is almost over, because you've just about given up.

On the outside you can make yourself look just peachy. You can look like the perfect love-child conceived as a cross-fertilisation between Mother Theresa, The Pope, and Ned Flanders. Maybe on the inside it's a different story altogether.

Here's the scary bit about all this:

Principle 3
What's on the inside will always come out.

If you're pretending on the outside, but never fixing the deep issues on the inside, then one day, you will be found out. Come on – you know it's true.

It's true in the Bible

Let me give you one last reason as to why Principle 3 always holds. **God says so!**

> **Numbers 32:23**
> ...be sure that your sin will find you out.

God actually promises that what's on the inside will always come out. And there are 2 good reasons why this is a sure thing:

1. God wants it to happen

God never likes it when we pretend. He always wants our outside to reflect our inside. His name will be honoured far more when there is no deception in how you are living. So God's plan for your life is that what's on your inside will always come out.

2. The devil wants it to happen

The devil always wants to catch people out. He always wants to do as much damage to God's kingdom as possible. One of the ways to do this is to expose hypocrites. So if you're pretending to be Christian on the outside, but secretly hanging onto sin on the inside, then Satan will work his hardest to make sure that those secret sins are exposed at just the

"God never likes it when we pretend"

right time to do maximum damage to your credibility. Because every time your credibility is compromised, then in the eyes of the world, God's credibility is compromised as well.

Don't get me wrong – God and the devil want **opposite** things in your life. God wants his kingdom to be built up by your life, and the devil wants God's kingdom to be pushed backwards by your life. But for very different reasons, both God and the devil want what's on your inside – to come out to the surface. God wants your sins to come to the surface so you can deal with them and turn away from them. The devil wants your sins to come to the surface because he wants you to be exposed as a hypocrite.

Now think about it. If exposing what's really going on inside you is something that both God and the devil want to happen in your life, does it make sense to you that it absolutely will happen?

If there are things that need to be changed, then the rest of this book is dedicated to helping you get it right on the inside. If there are changes that God is prompting you to make, then be open to his Spirit, and be determined to make them happen.

> If, on the other hand, you are genuinely opening your heart to the work of God's Holy Spirit...
> If you're letting God change and re-shape what you are like deep inside...
> If you are growing a character that is becoming more and more like Jesus himself...
> If you want God to grow you to be awesome on the inside...

Then Principle 3 holds forward a fantastic promise for you:

"What's on the inside will always come out."

> If you truly want God to grow you to be "awesome on the inside"... then the rest of this book is just for you! Let's start by seeing how these three principles work out in real life situations.

5 the three principles in action

A quick refresher of the three principles:

> **Principle 1. What's on the inside is more important than what's on the outside.**
>
> **Principle 2. To change your outside, work on your inside.**
>
> **Principle 3. What's on the inside will always come out.**

Let's have a look at four examples of how these principles work in everyday life...

1. How to live your life

Luke 6:47-49

"I will show you what he is like who comes to me and hears my words and puts them into practice. He is like a man building a house, who dug down deep and laid the foundation on rock. When the flood came, the torrent struck that house but could not shake it, because it was well built. But the one who hears my words and does not put them into practice is like a man who built a house on the ground without a foundation. The moment the torrent struck that house, it collapsed and its destruction was complete."

This is a well-known story about two blokes who each build a beach house. On the surface, the houses look the same. They both look brilliant on the outside. Hard to tell the difference. Because the difference lies under the surface. One house is built on solid rock – on a sure and unshakeable foundation – while the other one is built on the sand – absolutely no foundations under the surface to hold it secure.

Both houses look pretty good on the outside – until the storm comes. And when they're placed under pressure – that's when what's on the inside is exposed. The house built on a firm foundation withstands the storm – but the house built without a foundation is smashed to pieces, and ultimately destroyed.

It's not how good the houses looked that ultimately mattered. Both houses looked superb on the outside. What really made the difference was what you couldn't see. It was the foundations that were underneath.

This makes a lot of sense if you're about to build a house. But Jesus didn't tell the story to help us get our house-building right. He told the story to help us get our lives right.

Think about your life. What matters to God is not so much what you look like on the outside. What matters to God is growing your character on the inside. And the key to that is listening to what Jesus says, and doing something about it.

2. How to be a leader

Back in the Old Testament days, God wanted to choose a king to rule over his people. He wanted to raise up a leader who would faithfully minister to his people. God sent his prophet Samuel to anoint the new king that he had already chosen. God sent him to the house of a man called Jesse – and give him instructions to anoint one of Jesse's sons to be the new king.

Have a look at what happens when Samuel enters Jesse's place – and looks at his sons to see who would be the new leader over God's people.

> ### 1 Samuel 16:6
> *When they arrived, Samuel saw Eliab and thought, "Surely the LORD's anointed stands here before the LORD."*

The first of Jesse's sons that Samuel encounters is the oldest – Eliab. He looks good. Real good. He's tall – he's confident – his body language oozes self-confidence – he has "leadership" stamped all over him. Samuel thinks to himself *"Surely this is the one!"*

But God has other plans in mind!

> **1 Samuel 16:7**
> *"But the LORD said to Samuel "Do not consider his appearance or his height, for I have rejected him. The LORD does not look at the things man looks at. Man looks at the outward appearance, but the LORD looks at the heart."*

God is not fooled by your reputation. He is not dazzled by your abilities. It doesn't matter to him how good you look...

> *"Man looks at the outward appearance, but the LORD looks at the heart."*

What really matters to God is growing your character on the inside.

3. How to choose a date

How do you choose a boyfriend or a girlfriend? How do you find your soul-mate? How do you link up with the person who may well become your life-long partner? Do you find the most attractive one and chat them up at the party? Do you try sending a flirty text message? Do you get on the internet and find them in the catalogue of some online dating service? What do you really look for in a person who will be your girlfriend or boyfriend? And for them to choose you – do you have to have the right clothes, the right hairstyle, and the right jewellery?

> **1 Peter 3:3-4**
> *Your beauty should not come from outward adornment, such as braided hair and the wearing of gold jewellery and fine clothes. Instead, it should be that of your inner self, the unfading beauty of a gentle and quiet spirit, which is of great worth in God's sight.*

God says that true beauty is always on the inside. You can decorate yourself with every beautifying accessory known to humankind, but deep down, it's your character that will become the basis for forming a lasting and satisfying relationship.

If you want to be stunningly attractive to a godly young man or woman, what should you do? Here is God's answer – develop the characteristic that they will find irresistible! And what's that, I hear you say? Grow

"What matters to God is growing your character on the inside"

your character to be more and more Christlike! That's where true beauty lies. That's where lasting relationships are made. That's where you really want to be awesome.

4. How to get involved in ministry

God wants every Christian involved in ministry to others. Whatever your age, God has something in mind that you can do that's going to help someone else. There is at least one thing that God has equipped you to be good at. Somewhere along the line – you will discover your spiritual gifts so that you can genuinely be of service to others.

We live in a world where we are dazzled by people's abilities. We make heroes out of rock-stars and sporting legends. It can happen in the Christian world as well. The talented musician – the gifted preacher – the generous giver – can all be looked on as "someone really special". But God has something else in mind!

> *1 Corinthians 13:1-3*
> *If I speak in the tongues of men and of angels, but have not love, I am only a resounding gong or a clanging cymbal. If I have the gift of prophecy and can fathom all mysteries and all knowledge, and if I have a faith that can move mountains, but have not love, I am nothing. If I give all I possess to the poor and surrender my body to the flames, but have not love, I gain nothing.*

Even in Christian ministry, the same 3 principles hold true. It doesn't matter how many ministry gifts God has given you – if you don't have the Christlike character on the inside, then all your showy gifts achieve zippo – absolutely nothing!

Do you want to be used by God so that you're able to minister effectively to others? Then let God build your character deep down – so that you truly will be awesome on the inside.

What makes it all possible

Can I be changed on the inside? Absolutely! If you belong to Jesus, then God has placed his Spirit within you so that you will be changed from the inside!

> **Romans 8:10-11**
> *But if Christ is in you, your body is dead because of sin, yet your spirit is alive because of righteousness. And if the Spirit of him who raised Jesus from the dead is living in you, he who raised Christ from the dead will also give life to your mortal bodies through his Spirit, who lives in you.*

If you belong to Jesus, then the same Spirit who raised Jesus from the dead is at work in your body to change your character to become more like Jesus! Amazing! That's how you can be awesome on the inside! Right now, I want to challenge you as to whether you are ready to allow God to do spiritual surgery on your inside so that your character will be developed to become just like Jesus. What is it that needs to be changed on your inside, so that you will become the man or woman that God wants you to be?

In the rest of this book, I want to help you to grow your heart so that you will be changed from the inside out.

God wants you to grow a powerful heart.
God wants you to grow a prayerful heart.
God wants you to grow a passionate heart.
God wants you to grow a pure heart.
God wants you to grow a positive heart.
God wants you to grow a "pumping" heart.

God has big things to do in your life! He wants to rebuild you to make you **awesome on the inside**.

Are you ready?

a heart that is prayerful

section 2

"This book helped me answer many questions that I have faced recently. I learnt many new things about my awesome God – as well as about myself." **Melissa, Year 9**

6 the problem of feeling powerless

Sometimes, I feel powerless...

I guess there have been many times in my life when I've felt absolutely powerless. I've been in a situation where I realised that no matter what I did – there was no way I could change my circumstances. There was nothing I could do.

Years ago as I was driving my van – I suddenly realised that the traffic had banked up in front of me, and I hurriedly hit the brakes at full pressure. What I didn't realise at the time, was that there was some water lying on the road, so the moment I hit the brakes, I started skidding across the top of the water. In the millisecond I had to think about it, I realised that my brakes were having no effect whatsoever on the speed of my car, and my steering was having no effect whatsoever on the direction of my car. There was nothing I could do. I felt absolutely powerless.

One of the joys of my life was taking my family to the USA. My kids were in their teenage years, so we went to every theme park we could find. At *Magic Mountain*, the *Superman* ride had just opened. The world's fastest and highest ride (or so they said!). It looked pretty gut-wrenching, but in a spirit of fatherly leadership, I jumped in with my kids, and we were strapped in securely.

At that moment we started the most ferocious acceleration I have ever experienced, my life flashed before my eyes. All I could think of was "We're all going to die!" Because at that moment, I realised that I was totally powerless. There was nothing I could do to stop this devastating ride. The situation was completely outside my control.

Feeling powerless in the world

When you look at the world around you, it's pretty easy to feel powerless. It's a big world out there, and it has some big problems. There's just so many people – so many difficulties – so many complications. Things can simply feel too big . Millions of people are starving. What can I do? Is there **anything** I can do? And even if I did something, would it really make a difference?

The hole in the ozone layer. Global warming. Violence. Over-population. Terrorism. Starvation. War. Pollution. Racial prejudice. Gangs. Oppression. Poverty. Natural disasters. Slums. You name it. There are some big problems in this world. And it's really easy to feel overwhelmed by it all. I mean, seriously, is there **anything** I can really do that will make one scrap of difference?

If sometimes you feel powerless, then I don't blame you. We live in a world where it seems like there is a giant conspiracy to keep each individual powerless. And if you genuinely feel there **is** nothing that you can do, then you probably **will** do nothing.

And that's a horrible feeling!

Feeling powerless in your life

But you don't need to go out into the big bad world to feel powerless. There are many situations much closer to home, where you can feel like there is absolutely nothing that you can do.

Maybe your parents are getting more and more stressed with each other – you know they're drifting apart – and you desperately want everybody to be happy again – but anything you say seems to make it worse. You absolutely want things at home to change, but you know that you don't have the ability to **make** it change. Powerless! It's a horrible feeling.

Maybe you desperately want your friends to become Christians. You talk to them, you pray for them, you invite them to Christian things – but no matter what you do they seem as far away from Jesus as they ever have been. Powerless!

Perhaps you've hurt someone – you've done the wrong thing – you've said the wrong thing – and now you want to put things right. But they're not interested. They won't let you explain. They won't even let you apologise. There's nothing you can do. Powerless!

It might even be that one day someone took advantage of you. Made you do things you didn't want to do. As you think back on it, perhaps you feel you should have fought them off harder. But you didn't know what to do. You froze. You felt powerless.

That's a horrible feeling, isn't it? You can feel so helpless. You can feel so hopeless. You can feel so powerless. It can feel like there's absolutely nothing you can do that would make one scrap of difference. And when you feel that way, it robs you of all your energy. You feel paralysed. You do nothing.

You never have to be powerless again!

Here's the good news. Read it carefully. If you have the Spirit of God working in you – even though you might sometimes **feel** powerless – **you never have to be powerless again**. No matter what's gone wrong, there is always something you can do. There is always something you can achieve. There is always a way where you can make a difference. Because if you have Jesus in your life – then with him **all things are possible!**

Listen to what Jesus says:

> *Matthew 19:26*
> *"With man this is impossible, but with God all things are possible."*

POWERFUL

Here's what the apostle Paul discovered:

Philippians 4:13
"I can do everything through him who gives me strength."

That's right! When you have Jesus in your life – even though **you** might feel powerless, **Jesus is never powerless!** When you allow God to change you on the inside, then you never have to be powerless again! There is **always** something you can do. There is always something you can do that will **really work**. There is always something you can do that can change

"With God, all things are possible"

even the most desperate situations. If you belong to Jesus – then he has given you the most powerful weapon in the world. He has given you a weapon that can defeat every enemy. He has given you a weapon that can overcome every situation. He has given you a weapon that takes you to the awesome power of the very throne-room of God himself.

The most powerful weapon in the world – placed in your hands! Can you believe it? And that most powerful weapon is – **prayer!**

You don't think prayer is powerful? You don't think prayer works? You don't think that prayer can change things?

Well, read on – and ask that God will change you on the inside so that you will develop a prayerful heart.

7 the power of prayer – james

You're wondering whether prayer is really powerful? You find it hard to believe that it really works? You're not even sure whether it's worth praying?

I have a confession to make. I often feel like that! I'm not the world's champion pray-er. Some of my Christian friends tell me about the wonderful time they have praying – where they spend hour after hour delighting in God and being transformed by the never-ending flow of prayers that come from their lips. They tell me how glorious it is – how difficult it is for them to tear themselves away. I believe them – but it's never that easy for me. Sometimes I have to force myself to pray – it doesn't seem to come naturally – and my prayers are never that long.

As much as anybody else, I need to hear what God tells me about prayer in the Bible. So let me check again – why should we bother praying?

Pray because you need to!

What sort of time is the best time to pray?

1.   When things are bad

James 5:13a
"Is any one of you in trouble? He should pray."

Serious? That's it? This is what God is saying – no matter how bad things are going for you at the moment – however difficult things might be, no matter how bleak the situation you are facing or how hopeless it appears to you... God's word says there is something powerful that you can do. You are able to make a change even to the most horrific situation that you might face.

When things are going bad – when you're in trouble – there is something powerful that you can do. Pray!

2.   When things are going well

James 5:13b
"Is anyone happy? Let him sing songs of praise."

What if things are going well? You still pray! You sing songs of praise! Whatever situation you are in, God says there is something powerful that you can do. Something that will change you on the inside. Something that will change things on the outside.

Pray!

That's it? YES! That's it!

3.   When you're sick

What about if I'm sick and I don't feel like praying?

James 5:13b
"Is any one of you sick? He should call the elders of the church to pray over him and anoint him with oil in the name of the Lord."

Even when you're sick. Even when someone you love has a terrible illness. You are **never** powerless. There's **always** something powerful you can do.

Pray!

That's it? YES! That's it!

> I remember when I first got the phone call from my wife, Karen. She had undergone a routine breast examination, and they had called her back for a second check-up. I remember her words: *"Tim, I've got cancer"*
>
> All sorts of panic filled my head. All sorts of thoughts that I knew I could never say out loud. *"Does this mean my wife will die?"* *"Does this mean that there'll be years and years of medical treatment with no result?"* *"Does this mean that our life together has now changed for the worse – permanently?"*

What overwhelmed me was Karen's determination to pray. I was the one running around feeling helpless. Karen was committed to praying. And so were many of our friends. Yes – Karen had to undergo surgery – and still has to take all sorts of medication, **but God has healed her**. She has no more cancer. She is strong and healthy – a marvellous woman of God.

God doesn't guarantee that he will **always** heal – but whether he does or not – there is always something powerful that you can do – pray!

If you're in trouble... if things are going bad... if you're in a messy situation... if things look hopeless... or if things are going well... if you're on top of the world... if you're achieving success... if things are good and you're happy... if you're sick... if there's an illness... if there is someone you love who has something very serious wrong with them...

There is something powerful that God wants you to do. He wants you to pray. There's the first powerful reason for praying. We pray because we need it!

But is it any good? *(Good question!)* Does it have any effect? *(Ditto!)*

Pray because it works

James 5:15
"And the prayer offered in faith will make the sick person well; the Lord will raise him up. If he has sinned, he will be forgiven."

Now I know you've probably prayed for stuff and you haven't seen it happen. I certainly have. There are times when I find praying very frustrating when I'm not getting the answer that I really want. But God's word clearly says that when you're praying for the things that God wants you to pray for... it **will** be answered!

We need to have the boldness to pray that sickness will be healed. We need to have the boldness to pray that sins will be forgiven.

Now, you've got to be prepared to accept the answer that God gives. And maybe his answer isn't exactly what you're hoping for. In fact, sometimes his answer is very different from the one you are expecting. But do you have the faith to believe God when he says that your prayers that are offered according to his **will** will change lives? Sicknesses can be healed; the hurting can be restored; the oppressed can be liberated; sins can be forgiven. Your prayers make the difference.

> **James 5:16**
> *Therefore confess your sins to each other and pray for each other so that you may be healed. The prayer of a righteous man is powerful and effective.*

Did you get what God is saying? The weapon of prayer that he has given to you is both **powerful** and **effective**. Powerful – that means it will make things change; effective – that means it's worth doing because it will achieve a result.

> *"Hang on", you're saying, "there's got to be a catch here! There's got to be some small print with conditions and exclusions. There's got to be an asterisk with the words 'Conditions apply'. God can't really mean it when he says that prayer is both powerful and effective!"*

> *"Aha! I've spotted it! I've picked out the qualifying condition! It's right there in front of me! It says the prayer of a **righteous** man is powerful and effective."*

Well, that makes sense, doesn't it! You've got to be **righteous** before your prayers will be powerful and effective. *(That explains why I'm always missing out!)* How can I be righteous enough to pray prayers that really make a difference?

Good question! How can you be a righteous person? How can you have prayers that are both powerful and effective? What sort of a person can pray prayers that are both powerful and effective?

The answer, my friends, is in the next verse in James (which is in the next chapter of this book!)

8 the power of prayer – elijah ... and you!

What sort of a person can pray prayers that are both powerful and effective? A man like the Old Testament prophet Elijah!

> **James 5:17-18**
> *Elijah was a man just like us. He prayed earnestly that it would not rain, and it did not rain on the land for three and a half years. Again he prayed, and the heavens gave rain, and the earth produced its crops.*

Back into the time machine

To make sense of this, we've got to go way back to the Old Testament days. Hundreds and hundreds of years before Jesus was born. God's land of Israel had split into two separate nations –Israel and Judah. In the nation of Israel, they had some kings – some leaders – who were incredibly unfaithful to God. They led their people astray – turned them away from worshipping the one true God, and led them in a wild dance in chasing after false gods.

One of those wicked kings was named Ahab. Listen to this brief description of him from the First Book of Kings:

> **1 Kings 16:33**
> *Ahab... did more to provoke the LORD, the God of Israel, to anger than did all the kings of Israel before him.*

God had had enough. He decided to act in judgement upon that evil king and the land he ruled. God raised up his prophet Elijah and told him that he wanted him to pray that there would be no more rain on the land until the people had repented – given up their false gods – and had started following the only true and living God.

> **James 5:17**
> *Elijah was a man just like us. He prayed earnestly that it would not rain, and it did not rain on the land for three and a half years.*

Three and a half years without rain! And simply because one man prayed! God now arranges for a show-down between his prophet Elijah, and the wicked king Ahab. So in the third year of total drought, God arranges for a meeting between the two.

The Meeting with Ahab

> **1 Kings 18:1**
> *After a long time, in the third year, the word of the LORD came to Elijah: 'Go and present yourself to Ahab, and I will send rain on the land.'*

> **1 Kings 18:17-18**
> *"When he saw Elijah, he said to him, 'Is that you, you troubler of Israel?'*
> *'I have not made trouble for Israel,' Elijah replied. 'But you and your father's family have. You have abandoned the LORD's commands and have followed the Baals.'*

The Baals were the false gods that King Ahab had started worshipping. Elijah directly confronts him with his sin of abandoning the true God, and following after false gods.

The Contest

Now the people of Israel are in two minds. Sometimes they think about

following the only true God, but most of
the time, they abandon him. They start
following their own false gods that Ahab
had led them to. God tells Elijah to design
a contest to show once and for all that the
LORD is the only true God, and that anyone else is
an impostor who has no power to save.

God tells Elijah to assemble the whole community on Mount Carmel –
where there's going to be a show-down between the hundreds of prophets
of Baal, and the solitary prophet of God, Elijah.

1 Kings 18:19-24

*'Now summon the people from all over Israel to meet me on Mount
Carmel. And bring the four hundred and fifty prophets of Baal
and the four hundred prophets of Asherah, who eat at Jezebel's
table.' So Ahab sent word throughout all Israel and assembled the
prophets on Mount Carmel.*

*Elijah went before the people and said, 'How long will you waver
between two opinions? If the LORD is God, follow him; but if Baal
is God, follow him.' But the people said nothing. Then Elijah said
to them, 'I am the only one of the LORD's prophets left, but Baal
has four hundred and fifty prophets.'*

Under God's instructions, Elijah now designs a contest. The false prophets
will build an altar to their false god, and Elijah will build and altar to the
true God. Which God will prove themselves by sending fire to light their
altar? That will be the proof of which God is the real deal!

*'Get two bulls for us. Let them choose one for themselves, and let
them cut it into pieces and put it on the wood but not set fire to
it. I will prepare the other bull and put it on the wood but not set
fire to it. Then you call on the name of your god, and I will call on
the name of the LORD. The god who answers by fire--he is God.'
Then all the people said, 'What you say is good.'*

The Prophets of Baal

Read the vivid description of how the prophets of Baal got ready to hear from their "god".

1 Kings 18:25-29

Elijah said to the prophets of Baal, 'Choose one of the bulls and prepare it first, since there are so many of you. Call on the name of your god, but do not light the fire.' So they took the bull given them and prepared it. Then they called on the name of Baal from morning till noon. 'O Baal, answer us!' they shouted. But there was no response; no-one answered. And they danced around the altar they had made.

At noon Elijah began to taunt them. 'Shout louder!' he said. 'Surely he is a god! Perhaps he is deep in thought, or busy, or travelling. Maybe he is sleeping and must be awakened.' So they shouted louder and slashed themselves with swords and spears, as was their custom, until their blood flowed. Midday passed, and they continued their frantic prophesying until the time for the evening sacrifice. But there was no response, no-one answered, no-one paid attention.

There was no response, no-one answered, no-one paid attention. False gods – of any description – are kinda like that!

Elijah's preparation

Elijah now prepares his altar. And just to prove that he has no tricks up his sleeve, he gets the people to flood his altar with water – so there could be no way in the world that it could "accidentally" catch on fire.

> ## "Elijah had a simple faith in an awesomely powerful God"

1 Kings 18:30-35

Then Elijah said to all the people, 'Come here to me.' They came to him, and he repaired the altar of the LORD, which was in ruins. Elijah took twelve stones, one for each of the tribes descended from Jacob, to whom the word of the LORD had come, saying, 'Your name shall be Israel.' With the stones he built an altar in the name of the LORD, and he dug a trench round it large enough to hold two seahs of seed. He arranged the wood, cut the bull into pieces and laid it on the wood. Then he said to them, 'Fill four large jars with water and pour it on the offering and on the wood.'

'Do it again,' he said, and they did it again. 'Do it a third time,' he ordered, and they did it the third time. The water ran down around the altar and even filled the trench.

Elijah's prayer

Elijah had a simple faith in an awesomely powerful God. Look at his simple prayer. And look at the mighty way that God answered!

1 Kings 18:36-39

At the time of sacrifice, the prophet Elijah stepped forward and prayed: 'O LORD, God of Abraham, Isaac and Israel, let it be known today that you are God in Israel and that I am your servant and have done all these things at your command. Answer me, O LORD, answer me, so these people will know that you, O LORD, are God, and that you are turning their hearts back again.'

Then the fire of the LORD fell and burned up the sacrifice, the wood, the stones and the soil, and also licked up the water in the trench. When all the people saw this, they fell prostrate and cried, 'The LORD – he is God! The LORD – he is God!'

God's answer

Of course, the real answer to prayer was that the drought would end – that God would once again bless his people with abundance of rain.

> *1 Kings 18:41-45*
> *And Elijah said to Ahab, 'Go, eat and drink, for there is the sound of a heavy rain.' So Ahab went off to eat and drink, but Elijah climbed to the top of Carmel, bent down to the ground and put his face between his knees.*
>
> *'Go and look towards the sea,' he told his servant. And he went up and looked. 'There is nothing there,' he said. Seven times Elijah said, 'Go back.' The seventh time the servant reported, 'A cloud as small as a man's hand is rising from the sea.' So Elijah said, 'Go and tell Ahab, 'Hitch up your chariot and go down before the rain stops you.'*
>
> *Meanwhile, the sky grew black with clouds, the wind rose, a heavy rain came...*

Elijah must have been a righteous man. His prayer was both powerful and effective. Under God's instructions, he prayed that it would not rain –and it did not rain for over three years. Under God's instructions he prayed that God would answer with fire. And he did! Under God's instructions, he prayed that once again God would bless his people with rain. And God answered!

> *"Well,"* you're saying to yourself *"That's fine for Elijah! No doubt a mighty man! No doubt a righteous man. It's clear that his prayers are both powerful and effective. But I am nothing like that, I could **never** be like that."*

"God wants to develop in a you a heart for prayer"

You

Read again those verses from James that reflect on Elijah and his prayer. **And note carefully the first seven words!**

> *James 5:17-18*
> *Elijah was a man just like us. He prayed earnestly that it would not rain, and it did not rain on the land for three and a half years. Again he prayed, and the heavens gave rain, and the earth produced its crops.*

"Elijah was a man just like us." Can you believe it? In one sense he was no-one special. Just a servant of God striving to be faithful. Just someone who understood that he himself was weak, but that his God was so strong and so mighty. We see that Elijah prayed from his heart – and that God heard his prayer and answered his prayer.

"Elijah was a man just like us." Do you know what that means? **If Elijah can pray bold prayers that are both powerful and effective, then you can too!**

I struggle to believe this sometimes. I know it's all true. But sometimes I just don't pray.

I work hard, I organise, I plan, I prepare, I stay up late to get things finished, I push myself to the limit, I use my human wisdom, I think of clever answers, I try to invent a man-made solution, I use my creativity, I try to work out my own answers...

And sometimes I'm more like those prophets of Baal than I am like Elijah. Just racing around doing everything myself – rather than simply trusting the powerful God who loves to hear and answer my prayers.

What about you?

God wants to develop in you a heart for prayer. God doesn't just want you to be a person who prays. **He wants you to be a person OF prayer.**

God wants to build you to be awesome on the inside. The starting point? That you might ask him to grow in you a prayerful heart.

Are you game to ask him? Talk to him now. Go on – I promise I won't go away. I'll meet you a bit later in the next chapter.

a heart that is passionate
that is

section 3

"Wherever I am – at home, on the sporting field, or out with mates, I know that God wants me to be passionate about him." **Gilbert, Year 8**

9 the passion principle

Sometimes it matters to be passionate

There are some things in life that demand that you be absolutely 100% committed. Some things that you would never want to do in a half-hearted way. There are some things that if you don't do them with all your heart, you might as well not do them at all.

> It's the dance floor at the big concert. These are the lucky people who got in first and have crammed down the front – right in front of the stage. This is where the action is! This is the mosh pit!
>
> The band is thumping out the music. What's the mosh pit doing? People are standing there politely with their arms folded. Everyone is quiet, listening to the music. At the end of each song, people politely clap. You spot someone who is carefully passing a cup of tea to his friend as they enjoy the festivities.
>
> NO-O-O! That's not what a mosh pit is! Mosh pits have the whole crowd jumping up and down – waving their arms frantically – singing at the top of their voices – stage-diving, crowd-surfing, yelling and screaming and dancing around.
>
> You can't mosh in a quiet and dignified way! You've got to do it with all your heart!

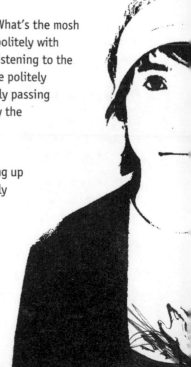

There are some things that if you don't do them with all your heart, you might as well not do them at all.

Playing in a sporting team works like that. If the team doesn't join in with all their heart – then it's probably not a team worth joining. There's no place on the sporting field for half-hearted efforts – where you just "go along with the motions" for a bare-minimum effort.

There are some things that if you don't do them with all your heart, you might as well not do them at all.

> ## "If you don't do it with all your heart, you might as well not do it at all"

Imagine your little child has gone missing. How much effort would you put into finding them? Can you imagine looking for them in a half-hearted way – not really caring whether you find them or not?

NO-O-O-O!!!! There are some things that if you don't do them with all your heart, you might as well not do them at all. You can't do them half measure! You've got to do them flat out. If you can't do them with commitment and passion – you may as well not do them at all!

Does it matter as a Christian

What about living as a Christian? Is that something you've got to be passionate about – absolutely whole-hearted – doing it with all your might? Or is it okay if you "just do it"?

Jesus said we've got to trust in him. You've got to obey him. You've got to follow him. But do I have to be excited about it? Isn't it okay if I 'just do it'? Do I really have to be passionate about it?

Here's the way it often goes. When you start out as a Christian everything is fantastic. Maybe you become a Christian quite young and everything is a buzz. It's new – it's fantastic – and you can't stop getting excited about it. You love going to your Bible study group, you invite everyone at your school to your youth group, you pray with your friends for hours, and you dream about your church camp for months before it is even on.

No-one has to encourage you to stick at it. You are on super-charged, high octane, adrenalin rush, caffeine concentrated, steroid Christianity! It is the biggest buzz and you are supremely passionate.

"You still do what Jesus wants – but not wholeheartedly"

You get a little bit older – college beckons – and things seem to change. You're still committed – you still want to follow Jesus – but it's not as much fun as it used to be. You're not quite as enthusiastic as you once were. Everything takes a bit more effort.

You still do what Jesus wants. But maybe not that wholeheartedly.

And it gets worse. By the time you're through your twenties and way into your fat-and-forties – man – you haven't got enthusiasm for anything! You've become a comfortable Christian.

By the time you're 40, you know how you like church and you don't want it to change. You've picked your favourite seat in church and you never sit anywhere else. And you'd like things done the way they've always been done because... that's the way they've always been done!

I remember when we changed the name of our summer youth camp from "KC" to "Impakct". It had always been called "KC" because the first time we held it, it was located at the beach-side town of Kiama. It was simply called "Kiama Camp" – or "KC". We hadn't been back to Kiama for over 10 years. The camp was long overdue for a change of name. When we eventually made the change, some of our radical, contemporary, "living on the edge" high-schoolers didn't like the idea of changing names. They wanted it to stay as "KC". Why? *"It's always been called KC".*

As you go on as a Christian, and maybe you've lost some of your enthusiasm, is that okay? Do you have to be passionate about following Jesus, or can you "just do it"

And maybe if you've lost some of your passion, how do you regain it?

The Passion Principle

Here is the Biblical principle that answers all those questions for us. It comes from Paul's letter to the Colossians.

> ### Colossians 3:23
> *Whatever you do, work at it with all your heart, as working for the Lord, not for men*

Note the 2 key guidelines for everything you do:

1.   Work at it with all your heart

You're never meant to do anything in a half-hearted way. God says "whatever you do, work at it with **all your heart**". 100% – boots and all – absolutely passionate!

Why should I?

2.   Because you're working for the Lord

You don't read your Bible because your youth leader said you should. You don't come to church because you've simply "got into the habit". You don't get involved in ministry to others "because it's expected of you." You don't obey your parents just so they won't get angry with you.

In everything you do, you work at it with all your heart – why?

You do it because you're working for the Lord!

> If it's your job to clean the toilets, you clean them like you're getting them ready for Jesus himself. You study hard at school like you're preparing your work for Jesus to inspect. You obey your parents like Jesus himself is giving you the commands. You live every moment of your being as if you are directly serving Jesus.

That's why it has to be flat out, passionate, "with all your heart"! You're doing it for Jesus!

You mean I've got to be whole-hearted for Jesus **all** the time?

Mark 12:28-30
One of the teachers of the law came and heard them debating. Noticing that Jesus had given them a good answer, he asked him, 'Of all the commandments, which is the most important?'

*"The most important one," answered Jesus, "is this: 'Hear, O Israel, the Lord our God, the Lord is one. Love the Lord your God with **some of** your heart and with **some of** your soul and with **some of** your mind and with **some of** your strength.'"*

Oops! Seems to be a little typographical error in there somewhere. I think we got some of the words wrong. Did you spot it? Let's have another try!

"Love the Lord your God with **all** your heart"

> *"Love the Lord your God with **most of** your heart and with **most of** your soul and with **most of** your mind and with **most of** your strength."*

Got it wrong again! Come on – you know what Jesus really said!

> *"Love the Lord your God with **all** your heart and with **all** your soul and with **all** your mind and with **all** your strength."*

If you're not following Jesus passionately – with **all** your heart and with **all** your soul and with **all** your mind and with **all** your strength – then Jesus says it ain't worth doing.

So how do you regain your passion if you think you've lost it somewhere along the way? *(that's the cue to turn to the next chapter!)*

10 four steps to a passionate heart

If you think you've lost some of your passion to follow Jesus, how do you get it back? What can you do so that you can truly grow a passionate heart? How do you regain your passion if you think you've lost it somewhere along the way?

Here are four steps – so that you really might become awesome on the inside.

Step 1: Hunger to be with God

Listen to the words of David:

> ### Psalm 130:5-7
> *"I wait for the LORD, my soul waits, and in his word I put my hope. My soul waits for the Lord more than watchmen wait for the morning... O Israel, put your hope in the LORD, for with the LORD is unfailing love and with him is full redemption."*

Like a watchman waits for the morning

Did you spot the passion of this guy who is absolutely desperate to be with his God? Look at the words he uses to describe how he really feels.

He is *"waiting for the Lord"*. Are you getting a picture of a man who is absolutely passionate to be with his Lord?

He is *"putting his hope in God's word"*. Trusting every word that God says.

But note carefully his third description of how he is feeling.

> *"My soul waits for the Lord more than watchmen wait for the morning"*

Back in those days, people lived in walled cities. During the day they would work outside the walls – out in the fields. But at night, all the citizens would come back in behind the city walls where they were secure for the night. To protect the city from any enemy invader, watchmen would patrol the city walls all night – keeping their eyes peeled for any potential attack.

There would be long nights. Dark. Cold. Lonely. Imagine how much the watchman would long for the morning! How desperate he would be to see those first rays of the sun filter over the horizon! How excited he would be to know that his shift was over – that a new day had dawned –and that the city was once again safe.

If you've ever had a sleepless night, you know how much you long for morning to come. Perhaps you've been out camping – and no matter how many times you twist and turn, you simply can't get comfortable – you can't sleep – and you're longing to see the first light of morning.

Can you imagine how much a watchman would long for the morning? David says that *"my soul waits for the Lord **more** than watchmen wait for the morning"* When you think *"I could sit down with my Bible and meet with God"* – are you hungry for that moment more than watchmen wait for the morning?

"God is hungry to meet with you"

Now, you might be thinking to yourself *"Why would anyone be desperate for that? I'm just meeting with God. I mean, I can pick up my Bible anytime. What's the big deal?"*

God is hungry to meet with you!

Here's something to think about. How does **God** feel when he thinks about spending time with **you**?

> ### Zephaniah 3:17
> The LORD your God is with you, he is mighty to save. He will take great delight in you, he will quiet you with his love, he will rejoice over you with singing.

Did you get what is going on for God when he thinks about the possibility of sitting down with you?

God says he takes great delight in you! Yes – you! God says he wants to "quiet" you – or "overwhelm" you with his love! Great! But the last line has the clincher – *"he will rejoice over you with singing"*

Can you imagine that? When God thinks about hanging out with you, he is "rejoicing over you with singing"!! Can you picture that? God is so keen to meet with you that he is singing with delight because of you! What a great picture!!

God is longing to meet with you. **How could you possibly not be longing to meet with him?**

Do you want to grow a passionate heart? Then be hungry to meet with God. Do it when you feel like it. Do it when you don't feel like it. And God will grow in you a passionate heart.

Step 2: Expect God to Answer

Listen again to David's words:

> **Psalm 5:3**
> *In the morning, O LORD, you hear my voice; in the morning I lay my requests before you and wait in expectation.*

God wants you to wait for his answer

David says that he lays his requests before God in prayer **and then he waits in expectation!**

Do you do that? When you pray, do you expect to see God answer that prayer? Or deep down are you expecting that he probably **won't** answer? Because if you're praying for something, and you're not **expecting** to see God's answer, then you're not gonna **get** God's answer!

> **"Are you expecting God to answer your prayers?"**

Test yourself. If you're praying for someone who is sick, are you expecting to see them get better? If you're praying that something that is lost will be found, are you expecting that you will find it? If you're praying for someone to become a Christian, are you expecting that you will see their life turn around?

Now you know God might have a different answer in mind. And you know that God will answer his prayer HIS way, not yours, but...

When you pray do you expect to see God answer that prayer? Or deep down are you expecting that he **won't** answer. Because if you're praying for something, and you're not **expecting** to see God's answer, then you're not going to **get** God's answer.

And do you know why?

> *Psalm 37:4*
> *Delight yourself in the LORD and he will give you the desires of your heart.*

God gives you the desires of your heart. If your words are saying "God, please answer this prayer" but deep down your heart is saying "But I don't really expect that you will answer" – then God knows what your heart is saying and according to Psalm 37 **"God will give you the desires of your heart"**. If you don't **expect** to see God answer your prayer, then you shouldn't be surprised when you don't **see** God's answer.

God wants you to have an expectant spirit

Are you picking up from all this that God wants you to have an expectant spirit? Now you know what the word "expectant" means. It's like an expectant mother. You know what that means. When someone is an expectant mother, that means that you know that something is growing

and developing, and you are fully expecting that a new human being will be born.

You are not expecting that that lump in your womb is a baby chimpanzee! You're not expecting it's a watermelon! Even though you can't **see** it yet, you are **expecting** that you will give birth to a brand new baby human being.

That's how you have an expectant spirit in prayer. You know that something is growing and developing – because you're praying about it. You can't yet see your answer from God, but you are **expecting** that you will see the answer from God.

A real key to growing a passionate heart is to expect to see God work. And here's a good reason why you can expect that.

> **Joshua 23:14**
> *... You know with all your heart and soul that not one of all the good promises the LORD your God gave you has failed. Every promise has been fulfilled; not one has failed.*

"Every promise has been fulfilled; not one has failed." Do you believe that? When you pray, do you expect that you will see God's answers? When you read your Bible, are you expecting that God will speak to you? When you meet up with your fellow Christians, are you expecting that you will be able to encourage and strengthen them in their day-to-day life?

When you go to church, are you expecting that God will speak to you? Are you expecting that God has a message for you? Are you expecting that you will be encouraged by being in God's family?

If you were genuinely expecting God to do big things at church, you wouldn't sit in the worst seats. You wouldn't stand around outside talking when everything had already started. You wouldn't be passing notes to your friends during the sermon. You would be front row, centre seat, your own Bible open, your pen in your hand, taking notes, joining in with all your heart at every opportunity!

If there was an open prayer or sharing time you wouldn't sit back and let everybody else be the only ones who come out the front and share what's on their heart. If there was an offering, and you were expecting that your church could be a real blessing to others, then you'd be giving with generosity. If you were expecting that God would use you in your day-to-day life to bring others closer to him, then you'd be looking for opportunities every day to say something to your friends about your faith in Jesus Christ.

But if you're not *expecting* God to do great things – don't be surprised if you don't get to see him *do* great things!

Imagine being part of a gathering of Christians where everyone showed up expecting God to answer their prayers, expecting to hear God speak personally to them from his word, where people gave generously with all their might, and where people were expecting to help and encourage each other, and to see God at work in their lives! Man – I'd love to be in that congregation! And if you're saying to yourself "My church isn't really like that" – then I have one question for you "Are you part of the problem, or part of the solution?"

Step 3: Praise God with everything you've got

Psalm 103:1
"Praise the LORD, O my soul; all my inmost being, praise his holy name"

This is one of David's songs. Sometimes when we sing, we sing directly to God himself. Sometimes when we sing, we are singing to encourage each other. Who is David talking to in this psalm?

"Praise the LORD, O my soul; all my inmost being, praise his holy name." He is talking to his own soul! He is talking to his inmost being! He is talking to himself! You can almost picture him saying: *"Hey – every single part of my body – I want your attention. Listen up, you arms! Come on – kidney and liver – I need you too. Even my toenails – I want you in on this. Every single section of my body – we're going to work together to praise God's name."*

Why is David able to praise God with absolutely everything?

> ### Psalm 103:1-5
> *Praise the LORD, O my soul; all my inmost being, praise his holy name. Praise the LORD, O my soul, and forget not all his benefits – who forgives all your sins and heals all your diseases, who redeems your life from the pit and crowns you with love and compassion, who satisfies your desires with good things so that your youth is renewed like the eagle's.*

You can praise God in so many ways. You praise him by yourself every time you pray. You praise God every time you obey him. You praise God every time you make a stand for him at your school or workplace. You praise him when you live for him. You praise him when you speak for him.

But wherever you praise God, and however you praise God,

"God wants to grow in you a passionate heart"

praise him *with all your soul,* and with all your inmost being. And when you come to church – when you come to your youth group – and you praise God together in song, praise him with all your soul and praise him with all your inmost being.

Now I know this would never happen at your church, but... ah... um... how can I put this delicately... "at a church I visited once" when the music was playing and it was time to sing God's praises, I saw people there with their mouths closed!

Aarrgghh!! How could you?

"I'm not into singing!" But are you into praising God?

"It's not my favourite song!" Hey – it's not for you – it's for God and to help the other people there praise God too!

"What would my friends think?" What would God think?

Can you see how God wants to build you to be awesome on the inside! He wants to grow a passionate heart in you.

Step 4: Proclaim God's Word Boldly

Let me introduce you to what is going on in Acts Chapter 4. Peter and John have healed a crippled man and they have proclaimed the message of Jesus. The authorities are not too impressed with this, so they are hauled in for interrogation. The community of believers prays for them to be released – and eventually they are set free. But when they are released, they are sternly warned to never speak publicly about Jesus again.

This is what they pray:

> ### Acts 4:29-31
> *'Now, Lord, consider their threats and enable your servants to speak your word with great boldness. Stretch out your hand to heal and perform miraculous signs and wonders through the name of your holy servant Jesus.' After they prayed, the place where they were meeting was shaken. And they were all filled with the Holy Spirit and spoke the word of God boldly.*

What was their prayer after they were released? What was the community of believers passionate to see happen?

> *'O Lord, please protect us from the evil authorities'?? 'Lord, help us to live contentedly, and not to upset our community by being too forceful'??*

NO-O-O-O!! Look at what they actually prayed!

> *'Now, Lord, consider their threats and enable your servants to speak your word with great boldness.'*

They asked God to enable them to speak with **even greater boldness!** And when they had finished praying, God answered their prayer immediately!

After they prayed, the place where they were meeting was shaken. And they were all filled with the Holy Spirit and spoke the word of God boldly.

That's how bold God wants you to be! And deep down, that's probably how bold you really want to be!

You don't want to be some mealy-mouthed, wishy-washy, luke-warm, watered-down, no name, low octane, unleaded, bargain basement, go-lo, self service, bottom of the barrel, bare minimum Christian!

God wants you to be an on-fire, charged up, red hot, bold as brass, high octane, ready-for-anything passionate disciple!

God wants to grow in you a passionate heart!

> **"God wants you to be an on-fire, charged up, red hot, bold as brass, high octane, ready-for-anything passionate disciple"**

One last word on all this passion stuff...

It really matters. You can't just "do" Christianity. You need to do it **with all your heart**. And it can get really dangerous when you don't.

In the Old Testament, there are short sentences that summarise every one of the various kings of Israel and Judah. A comment that is made on each of God's leaders. They usually tell you stuff like: how old they were when they became king; how long they reigned for; their family background; and how they did at following God.

A king you've probably never heard of is "Amaziah". But have a look at the summary description of his leadership:

2 Chronicles 25:1-2

Amaziah was twenty-five years old when he became king, and he reigned in Jerusalem for twenty-nine years. His mother's name was Jehoaddin; she was from Jerusalem..."

So far, so good. But let's just read one more sentence...

... He did what was right in the eyes of the LORD, but not wholeheartedly.

Did you get what was said about him? *"He did what was right in the eyes of the LORD..."* and then the Bible adds those three words which change everything. *"... **but not wholeheartedly"**.*

Could that description ever be used of you? *"You did what was right in the eyes of the Lord – **but not wholeheartedly"***

Amaziah ended up walking away from God completely. He *kind of* did the right thing, but his heart was not in it. He was not on fire for his God. He did not bother to grow a passionate heart.

The final words on this subject belong to Jesus. Here he answers the question "What is the greatest commandment?" Read this through slowly, and notice how Jesus keeps repeating the word "all". Do you get the idea that he's trying to teach us something?

Mark 12: 30

*'Love the Lord your God with **all** your heart and with **all** your soul and with **all** your mind and with **all** your strength.'*

If you truly want to follow Jesus, ask him in prayer now, that he will grow in you a passionate heart. Tell him that you want to be committed to him – absolutely wholeheartedly – for the rest of eternity.

a heart that is pure

section 4

" This book issues me a much-needed call – to be genuine, to let God cut me to the core and then rebuild me." **Ingrid, Year 12**

11 stop scoring goals for the Opposition

The problem of a divided heart

You've probably never thought of what it means to have a "divided heart". You may never have heard the term before. But a divided heart is the opposite of having a pure heart. A divided heart is the barrier to the thrill of having God grow you as Awesome on the Inside.

It doesn't work in sport!

Imagine you're playing on a football team. You're there with all your mates. It's a fierce and incredibly close match. Your team is under a lot of pressure. And then you notice something incredibly strange. One of your own defenders deliberately passes the ball to the opposition and helps them score a goal against you.

You can't believe it! One of your own team! You go up to him and yell at him *"What did you do that for?"* *"I dunno,"* he replies *"he was me mate!"*

You shake your head and get back to the game. Your team has managed to claw a goal back. It looks like it's heading for a draw. And then, in the dying minutes of the game, this same bozo on your team gets control of the ball, turns around, and starts heading towards your own goal, dribbles around every other defender, and belts the ball **in your own goal** past your own bewildered goalkeeper.

"What are you doing?" you scream at him!

> **"You can't keep scoring goals for the opposition"**

"I just wanted to score a goal!" he yells back.

In frustration you yell, *"But you scored it against your own team!"*

His answer? *"It was easier. It was fun"*

You can't have someone on your team who scores goals for the opposition. You can't have someone playing on your team who has a divided heart.

It doesn't work in love

Imagine you've got a boyfriend. (Guys, you'll just have to reverse this story!) He treats you special. Buys you things, cares for you, tells you you're the only girl in the world for him. And he's a good kisser.

You're his girl. He's your man. Everything looks rosy.

And then one night you catch him rolling around on the lounge passionately snogging your best friend.

> *"What are you doing?"* you blurt out.
> His reply?
> *"Hey – I wanted to kiss someone. And you were busy."*
> *"But you were kissing my best friend!"*
> He doesn't even try and hide it.
> *"Of course I did – and I want to tell you – it was **brilliant**"*

You can't have a relationship with someone who has a cheating heart.
You can't have a relationship with someone who has a divided heart.
You can't have a relationship with someone who scores goals for
the opposition.

It doesn't work with Jesus

Let's say you're a Christian. You've committed your life to following Jesus. You've dedicated every moment of your existence to praising his name and living his way. You know that he is the only one who can bring you true satisfaction. And you know that he wants you to have a pure and clean heart.

But you've got these porn videos. And every now and again, when no-one else is watching, you pull one out, and just for a short moment you don't care what Jesus thinks. You've forgotten all about having a pure heart.

> "Aren't you meant to have a heart for Jesus?"
> "Yeah – but it felt good!"

You can't be a faithful Christian and hang onto a cheating heart.
You can't be a faithful Christian and hang onto a divided heart.
You can't bring honour to Jesus if you're scoring goals for the opposition.

The Secret Sins

Maybe for you it's not porn. Maybe it's something else. But is there something there that you're hanging onto, and you're not dealing with, and you're not giving up, and you're not confessing to God? Is there some habit that you've got into, or some sin that you're stuck in which is dragging you away from having an undivided heart in following Jesus?

> ## "Learn how to grow an undivided heart, so you can become an undivided disciple"

Is there something that is going on in your life – that maybe no-one even knows about – which is stopping you having a pure heart in following Jesus?

Is there an area of your Christian life where you keep scoring goals for the opposition?

> Stuff you do.
> Stuff you say.
> Stuff you watch.
> Stuff you think about.

Now don't get me wrong. I know you're a good person (otherwise you wouldn't be reading this book!) And I'm not pretending that I'm the wise-old-youth-leader-who's-never-sinned-and-even-if-I-did-it-was-so-long-ago-that-I-can't-remember!

I know there are things in **my** life too that aren't the way they're meant to be. I'm not pretending to be the all perfect whiter-than-white youth leader who's eliminated every sin in my life. There's stuff that I do – there's stuff that I say – there's stuff that I think about that does not bring honour to the name of Jesus.

> If you could examine my life, you'd see times when I did not have a pure heart.
> If you could check deep inside of me, you'd see times when I had a divided heart.
> If you knew me as well as God knows me, you'd see times where I was scoring goals for the opposition.

We're in this together. Each one of us needs to be challenged by God to grow a pure heart. Each one of us needs to cry out to God so that he will build us to be truly Awesome on the Inside.

This is the scariest one

Right now, there might be a problem. You might be thinking to yourself "I don't want to read this". You may be very tempted to skip to the next section and read a "safer" area about growing as God's child.

But here's the scary bit. Even though you might not **want** to hear all this, there's a part of you that knows that you **need** to. And it's scary because when you read these chapters, then you know that if you're gonna be honest about following Jesus, things will have to change.

One more reason that all this is a bit scary. If you do not grow a heart that is pure – if you keep trying to follow Jesus with a divided heart, then your own heart might lead you to give up on Jesus altogether.

> **Hebrews 3:12**
> *"See to it, brothers, that none of you has a sinful, unbelieving heart that turns away from the living God."*

C'mon, let's work together on this. Let's work out how each one of us can really be someone with integrity. Let's hang in there so we can train our hearts to be pure. Let's learn how to grow undivided hearts, so that each one of us can become an undivided disciple.

Let's go to God's word together and see if we can stop scoring goals for the opposition.

12 joseph and the desperate housewife

Joseph

I want to look with you at Joseph. Not Joseph, the husband of Mary, but a Joseph who lived 1500 years before Jesus was born. Joseph – who had 11 brothers. Joseph who was given a multi-coloured coat by his father.

"Oh... **that** Joseph!"

Yep – that's the one. The *Joseph and the Amazing Technicolour Dreamcoat* Joseph!

You probably know the story. If anyone had a reason to turn away from God, it was Joseph. He had been miserably treated. He was attacked by his brothers and left for dead. He was sold by his brothers as a slave. He ended up as a slave in Egypt – stuck in a foreign country and removed from the fellowship of God's people. He would have felt lonely. He would have felt rejected.

Let's pick up the story in Genesis 39.

Genesis 39:1-4

Now Joseph had been taken down to Egypt. Potiphar, an Egyptian who was one of Pharaoh's officials, the captain of the guard, bought him from the Ishmaelites who had taken him there. The LORD was with Joseph and he prospered, and he lived in the house of his Egyptian master. When his master saw that the LORD was with him and that the LORD gave him success in everything he did, Joseph found favour in his eyes and became his attendant. Potiphar put him in charge of his household, and he entrusted to his care everything he owned."

The desperate housewife

We can see in the above passage that Joseph has been bought as a slave, and placed in the household of Potiphar – an important Egyptian official. Because Potiphar was often busy with government business, he would frequently be away for long periods of time. Because Joseph was so reliable and trustworthy, Potiphar left him in charge of his entire household while he was away. Whenever this occurred, Joseph was left alone at home with Potiphar's gorgeous wife.

> **Genesis 39:6-7**
> *Now Joseph was well-built and handsome, and after a while his master's wife took notice of Joseph and said, 'Come to bed with me!'*

Hang on! Hold the phone! This sounds like every fella's dream! I know some guys who spend endless hours trying to think of the right line to get a girl interested in them. In the Genesis 39 account, there's a luscious woman – all alone with Joseph in the house – and she says to him *"Come to bed with me!"*

Is this all your dreams come true?

"If your dream involves sin – it's a nightmare"

If your dream involves sin – then it is a nightmare. Sometimes things that look so attractive can be there to destroy you!

> It's like a high-cholesterol-overweight-high-blood-pressure-heart-bypass candidate looking at the gi-normous piece of chocolate cream bavarian pie.
>
> It looks terrific, but it will destroy him.

It's like taking the ultimate thrill of a bungee-jump with a rope that nobody has checked. Exciting – but deadly.

It's like a child wanting to play with the pretty sparks that are coming out of the old electric toaster. If no-one stops the child, then the toast ain't the only thing that's gonna get burnt...

Sin will *always* look attractive – but it will *always* destroy you. It will always turn your heart away from God. If it was really going to be good for you, God would say, *"Yep – I want you to do it."*

So here is Joseph, being tempted to have a sexual encounter with someone he is not married to. Sure – we know it happens every day on the TV soaps, but Joseph knows it is against God's great plan for sex. And he is not just tempted only once! In verse 10 we read that she kept this pressure up day after day!

> **Genesis 39:10**
> *And though she spoke to Joseph day after day, he refused to go to bed with her or even to be with her.*

Standing up for God has its cost

Joseph was determined to obey God. He was committed to being a person of integrity. He refuses to go to bed with someone he is not married to.

Does this mean that when you decide to do the right thing that you'll be hugely rewarded and live happily ever after? Unfortunately, not always. Sometimes standing up for God can involve a heavy cost. Sin has a way of being terribly unfair.

> **Genesis 39:11-20**
> *One day he went into the house to attend to his duties, and none of the household servants was inside. She caught him by his cloak and said, 'Come to bed with me!' But he left his cloak in her hand and ran out of the house.*
>
> *When she saw that he had left his cloak in her hand and had run out of the house, she called her household servants. 'Look,' she*

said to them, 'this Hebrew has been brought to us to make sport of us! He came in here to sleep with me, but I screamed. When he heard me scream for help, he left his cloak beside me and ran out of the house.'

She kept his cloak beside her until his master came home. Then she told him this story: 'That Hebrew slave you brought us came to me to make sport of me. But as soon as I screamed for help, he left his cloak beside me and ran out of the house.'

When his master heard the story his wife told him, saying, 'This is how your slave treated me,' he burned with anger. Joseph's master took him and put him in prison, the place where the king's prisoners were confined.

Joseph does what is right – and ends up being accused of rape and thrown into prison. Often there are no rewards when you decide to be a person of integrity. But you don't do what's right because of the reward – you do it because it is right. You do it because it helps your heart to be pure.

You do it because you don't want to score goals for the opposition.

"You don't do what's right because of the reward – you do it because it's right"

Joseph makes four decisions that helped to keep his heart pure. Four safety barriers to help guard his heart. If you want to grow a pure heart as you follow Jesus, check out these four safety barriers in Chapter 13.

13 four safety barriers to protect your heart

Before Joseph ran away from this sin, he made three statements – and then took one action. And if you want to grow a pure heart – then these are four very important strategies to pay attention to. Four very important steps to learn. Four ways to grow a pure heart. Four safety barriers to protect your heart.

Genesis 39:8-9

"With me in charge," he told her, "my master does not concern himself with anything in the house; everything he owns he has entrusted to my care. No one is greater in this house than I am. My master has withheld nothing from me except you, because you are his wife. How then could I do such a wicked thing and sin against God?"

Let's check out Joseph's three statements – and his one action. And let's learn the four safety barriers to protect your heart.

Safety Barrier 1: "I will not let others down"

Look back at **Genesis 39:8-9**.

"...everything he owns he has entrusted to my care.... My master has withheld nothing from me except you, because you are his wife..."

Joseph knows that if he sins in this way, he will let down the person who has trusted him with everything. He will let down Potiphar himself.

Of course, Joseph didn't have to look far to see someone else whom he was letting down. That's right—Potiphar's wife herself. If your sin ever involves someone else – you are certainly letting them down!

Compromise is always like that. When you give in – even in your private sin – there is somebody else whom you are letting down. We stand or fall with each other. Every time I compromise in some area of my Christian life – I am letting you down. Every time you compromise in your Christian life, you are letting me down. Christian integrity is like that. When one person abandons it – all of us suffer.

"Sin always lets someone else down"

You always let someone down.

If your parents are away for the weekend, and you break their trust by doing a whole stack of things that you know are wrong, then whether your parents ever find out or not, you still let them down. You break the trust that they have in you.

If you get involved sexually long before you are ready for it, there is always "someone else" that you let down. And you might let down someone that you haven't even met yet! Think about it. If you get involved sexually with someone who you're not married to, then you are letting down *your* future marriage partner. God wants you to keep yourself for that one right partner. So don't let them down even before you've met them!

When any one of us lets our integrity cave in, then a whole host of people are let down. That's the way it works in any team. If one team-member isn't pulling their weight, the whole team suffers.

Have you ever heard of a well-known "tele-evangelist" letting the team down by calling on others to run away from sin, but they themselves get caught out in an illicit sexual relationship? Or having asked for generous contributions from so many – to help people who are really badly off – have you ever heard of anyone who was "found out" for having their hand in the till?

Sadly, this sometimes happens. And when someone well-known loses their integrity, then the integrity of **every Christian** drops a little as well. Suddenly the world thinks less of us. Suddenly the world thinks less of Jesus. When one person sins, someone else is always let down.

> I had an acquaintance who was a youth minister. He worked with young teenagers. He had a thriving and growing youth ministry at his church. And then one day I heard he had been arrested on multiple charges of molesting children. He was subsequently convicted and imprisoned. This was horrendous for everyone who was involved.
>
> What do you think happened to all those young lives when the man they looked up to – their youth minister – was convicted of sexually abusing children? What did it do to their faith? What did it do to their youth group?

The words of Jesus are hauntingly true:

> **Matthew 26:31**
> *Then Jesus told them, "This very night you will all fall away on account of me, for it is written: 'I will strike the shepherd, and the sheep of the flock will be scattered.'*

This is Safety Barrier Number 1. Use it to guard your heart so that you do not stray away from being pure. When you are tempted to disobey Jesus, make the decision that you will not let others down. Because I can assure you, when you compromise your principles for a moment of pleasure, you **always** let someone else down.

Joseph's first statement: **"I will not let others down"**. Make it your first statement as well.

Safety Barrier 2: "I will not let myself down"

Look back at **Genesis 39:8-9**.

> *"How then could **I** do such a wicked thing?"*

Maybe you have a sin that is so private that absolutely no-one knows about it. But when you lose your integrity – you let yourself down – and you have to live with that. I know. I have done this myself.

Be honest with yourself. No matter what standard you have, you know how you feel when you break your own standard. When you go lower than you've gone before. When you **feel** lower than you've felt before.

You know what it feels like when you've done the wrong thing. You know what your failure feels like. You know the heaviness of your guilt. Even if no-one else ever finds out, you know you have let yourself down.

This is Joseph's second safety barrier – when he says, "I will not let myself down". You can make it a safety barrier for yourself as well. When you are tempted, be determined that you will not lower yourself. Remind yourself of what that guilt feels like. Remind yourself of what that failure feels like. Determine before God that you refuse to go again down that path.

Safety Barrier 3: "I will not let God down"

Look back at **Genesis 39:8-9**.

> *"How then could I do such a wicked thing **and sin against God?**"*

Joseph made a conscious decision not to let anyone down. Joseph made a conscious decision not to let himself down. But in his third statement, he trusts in his strongest safety barrier – "I will not let God down"

Because if something is not right – it is not right against God. Ultimately, our sin is not just against another person – our sin is against God. It was our sins that nailed Jesus to that tree. He is the one we will answer to. No matter

> **"If something is not right – it is not right against God"**

how enticing a particular sin is, your best safety barrier is to make a stand that you will not let God down. Because you know he will never let you down!

Safety Barrier 4: "Run!"

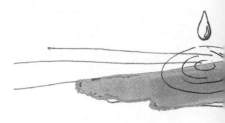

Joseph made three bold statements:

>*"I will not let others down."*
>*"I will not let myself down."*
>*"I will not let God down."*

And then he takes one decisive step. One action to remove himself from such temptation. One final safety barrier to protect his heart.

>**Genesis 39:12**
>*She caught him by his cloak and said, "Come to bed with me!"*
>*But he left his cloak in her hand and **ran** out of the house.*

He ran! He fled! He got the heck out of there!

And you know what – if only we could take that one decisive step when dealing with strong temptation! So much pain – so much misery – so much sin could be avoided if we simply took this crucial fourth safety barrier!

God wants us to flee – God wants us to run away from sin – God wants us to run straight back into his arms – cos he is there longing for us to return.

>If you want to have a pure heart...
>If you want to have an undivided heart...
>If you want to stop scoring goals for the opposition...

... then run clean away from the temptation that will drag you back into sin, and maybe drag you away from following Jesus.

The Bible is full of great examples of how to "flee" or "run" from danger.

Run from sexual sin

1 Corinthians 6:18

*"**Flee** from sexual immorality. All other sins a man commits are outside his body, but he who sins sexually sins against his own body."*

You know the things that will tempt you sexually. You know when you are placing yourself in a dangerous situation. God has some very simple advice. Flee! Run right away!

There was a bloke who owned a small trucking firm, and he was looking to employ a new driver. Three drivers had applied for this position, and they were all nervously sitting in the waiting room. One by one they were called in for their interview.

When the first bloke came out, the other two checked with him *"What did he ask you?"*

"He only asked one question. He asked me how close I could safely drive one of his trucks near the edge of a cliff."

"What did you say?"

"I said I could get one of his trucks to within 3 metres of the edge of a cliff".

"Was that good enough?"

"Don't think so. I didn't get the job."

The second bloke goes in, and was asked the same question. He answered *"I could get it to within one metre."* But apparently that wasn't good enough either. He didn't get the job.

The last bloke goes in. The boss looked at him and asked his standard question. *"If you were driving one of my trucks, how close could you safely drive it near the edge of a cliff?"*

His reply? *"If I were driving one of your trucks, I wouldn't go anywhere near the edge of a cliff!"* He got the job!

Sometimes we like to see how close we can get to a sin without actually sinning. But this is dangerous territory. People who hang around the edge of a cliff sometimes fall over. The Bible is clear. Stay **well away** from any area of danger. Flee! Run!

> ## "People who hang around the edge of a cliff sometimes fall over"

Run from worshipping anything else

> *1 Corinthians 10:14*
> *"Therefore, my dear friends, **flee** from idolatry."*

Idolatry is simply when you place anything else ahead of God. Idolatry is pushing God out of his rightful spot as number one in our lives, and spending our time and energy chasing something or someone else.

If you don't want to follow the one true God, there are any number of weird and wonderful religions that can present you with a false god. But idolatry can simply involve placing your success at number one, or valuing your friends more than you value Jesus, or chasing after pleasure, or comfort, or anything else that is not the one and only God.

So don't hang around waiting to be tempted. The Bible is clear. Flee! Run!

Run from being greedy

> *1 Timothy 6:10-11*
> *For the love of money is a root of all kinds of evil. Some people, eager for money, have wandered from the faith and pierced themselves with many griefs. But you, man of God, **flee** from all this, and pursue righteousness, godliness, faith, love, endurance and gentleness.*

Pretty straightforward really. How do you deal with the temptation to be greedy and spend your life chasing after money and the things it can buy? Simple! Flee! Run right away! Use your money and your possessions to honour God. But run away from the temptation to spend it selfishly and simply want more and more!

Run from sinful peer pressure

> **2 Timothy 2:22**
> "**Flee** the evil desires of youth, and pursue righteousness, faith, love and peace, along with those who call on the Lord out of a pure heart."

There will never be a shortage of "friends" who are keen to lead you down the wrong path. And while it's important to hang-in with your friends who need to find out more about Jesus, the Bible is clear on what you should do when they want you to join in something that is wrong. Flee! Run right away!

"Stay well away from the edge of the cliff"

These are Joseph's four safety barriers. Safety barriers that God has placed there to guard your heart. In whatever situation you are facing at the moment – can you make these your four safety barriers as well?

1. "I will not let others down"
2. "I will not let myself down"
3. "I will not let God down"
4. Run!

Running clear away from temptation can seem hard. And there is a dangerous alternative that will try to stop you! Read on!

14 the problem of "hanging around"

The alternative strategy

There is, of course, an alternative to "running" or "fleeing" from temptation. It's a strategy that we all use, but frankly, it's not very helpful. In fact, if we keep using this alternative strategy, we are **sure** to end up in more and more sin.

But you need to know about this alternative strategy. You need to know the dangers of it. And you need to know how hard it will make it for you to grow a pure heart. The opposite of "running away" is "hanging around". You can either "run away" from danger, or you can "hang around" danger. You have to pick one or the other! You can't do both!

And it will make a difference which one you pick. If there is a fallen electricity wire outside your house — and it is still "live" — it could make an enormous difference to the length of your life whether you choose to "run away" or "hang around"! Little kids will hang around and watch the pretty sparks. But part of growing in adult wisdom is knowing when to get the heck out of there!

The same is true of temptation. The opposite of running away is "hanging around." You cannot do both at the same time. See if you can spot the difference:

> You're determined to diet and lose weight. There's a big slice of double-chocolate cream Bavarian pie in the fridge.
> *Hanging around* means you keep it in the fridge "just to look at".
> *Running away* means you throw it in the bin.

There's an internet website that you know you shouldn't be looking at.

Hanging around means you close the page, but you keep it book-marked in case you need it again.

Running away means that after you close the page, you set up a control that won't allow you to go back there, and you make yourself accountable to a trusted Christian friend.

You have some CD's and computer programmes that you have illegally copied.

Hanging around means that you stop using them, but you store them on your shelf, and leave them on your hard drive.

Running away means that you throw out the CD's and erase them from your hard drive.

Do you get the difference between running away and hanging around? You need to check carefully which strategy you are currently using to deal with temptation. There might be some things that you need to change. Because only one of these strategies will help you to grow a pure heart. The other strategy could possibly lead you away from Jesus.

Only one of these strategies is a safety barrier which will guard your heart. The other is the "edge of the cliff" which can only lead to problems.

And here's some wisdom that you can put into action in every area of your life – *"Stay right away from the edge of the cliff!"*

"You can either 'run away' or 'hang around'. You can't do both!"

Think it through

Can you take a moment just to think through your life? Just by yourself. No-one else will know your thoughts. I'll be here to guide you – but even I will have no idea of what you're going to think about. It'll just be between you and God.

Can you think of areas in your life where your heart is not pure? Parts of your character where is your heart divided? Situations where you are dangerously close to the edge of the cliff? What temptations do you need to run from? Where are you scoring goals for the opposition?

You have two choices – to hang around, or to run away. Now – here's the trap: If you keep these thoughts to yourself – and never let anyone else know the struggle you are going through, you are probably still hanging around. Because the sins you never admit to, are the ones that you will never run from. If you want to run away, then make yourself accountable to a Christian whom you trust. Let them know you need help. Ask them to walk with you so that you don't have to face it alone.

And if you're serious about running away from temptation, and running back to God, here is some great news from the Bible:

> **1 John 1:7-9**
> *But if we walk in the light, as he is in the light, we have fellowship with one another, and the blood of Jesus, his Son, purifies us from all sin. If we claim to be without sin, we deceive ourselves and the truth is not in us. If we confess our sins, he is faithful and just and will forgive us our sins and purify us from all unrighteousness.*

Read through that last sentence again.

> *If we confess our sins, he is faithful and just and will forgive us our sins and purify us from all unrighteousness.*

If you are serious about coming back to God, then he is also serious about taking you back. He loves you so much and his forgiveness is bigger than any sin that you or I could ever dream up. His arms are open just waiting for you. So don't hold back on him. God can fix any broken heart – but you've got to give him all the pieces!

And just in case you're thinking of continuing to hang around — and not deal with the difficult stuff in your life — here is a warning from the Bible that we started with a few chapters ago:

> **Hebrews 3:12**
> *See to it, brothers, that none of you has a sinful, unbelieving heart that turns away from the living God.*

Come on — God wants you back. Why don't you take a moment now to sort things out with him? Talk to God in prayer. Determine to place those safety barriers in place. Catch up with a trusted Christian friend whom you know can help you.

God absolutely wants you to grow a pure heart. He absolutely wants you to become Awesome on the Inside!

"God's forgiveness is bigger than any sin"

a heart that is positive

15 three steps to a negative heart

Have you ever noticed how easy it is to be negative? It's so much simpler to complain about something that's wrong, than to encourage something that's right. It's the crazy sort of world that we live in.

When you're in a shop and you're not exactly getting excellent service, our first instinct is to grumble or complain.

When the weather isn't exactly the way that we want it, it's so easy to have an entire conversation full of negative comments about the weather!

When things at church aren't quite the way you like, it can be very tempting to complain about it in all your conversations that night.

If your school, or your youth group, or your small home group, or your Christian friends don't quite hit the mark – then watch out! It can be the easiest thing in the world to have a giant whinge session.

"Have you heard this one?" Usually heard when you're commenting on someone in a teensy little negative way. "Well, he's not a bad sort of a bloke, but..." And what follows the "but" is a catalogue of everything you don't like about the person.

It's so much easier to notice something that's negative rather than to search for the thing that's positive. It's so simple to pay someone out rather than building them up. And you might want to ask, "What's the harm in that? We're only having a bit of fun!"

Here's where it matters. God wants you to grow a heart that is positive,

"We feel we have the right to be negative towards others"

rather than a heart that is negative. And everything you say will either make your heart more positive, or more negative. And while it's easy to joke in a negative way; while it's not hard to think of funny put-downs; and while it's "clever" to blurt out some cutting sarcasm; there is always someone who is hurt by this. It can be incredibly dangerous and destructive to grow a negative heart.

Here are three dangerous steps to avoid.

Step 1: "Because I feel hurt I have a right to be negative"

Let's be honest. People do all sorts of hurtful things to us. Maybe you were treated badly when you were a kid. Perhaps you were mercilessly bullied when you were at school. Maybe the lady down the street is gossiping about you. Even your best friend might have just let you down. A member of your own family might have just said incredibly unkind things to you.

Or maybe just something really bad has happened. Someone you love has died. Your finances might have taken a nose-dive. Someone has turned against you and you don't even know why.

Or perhaps you're not treated that fairly. No-one else at home pulls their weight. Everyone expects too much of you. You might be taken for granted. Or used. Or abused.

This can be a pretty hurtful world. Everyone of us feels hurt at some stage. Let's admit it – sometimes life sucks. And here's the bit that feels unfair – you often have no choice in whether you get hurt or not. Getting hurt just seems to be part of the deal of living in a world that is infected by sin. No-one escapes it. You will be hurt if you're a president or a peasant; a business person or a pre-schooler; rich or poor; super-cool or super-geek. No-one escapes.

And of course, when you feel hurt, you probably feel like you have the right to be negative. But here's the problem – if **all** of us feel hurt at some stage – and **all** of us feel like we have the right to be negative – can you see the recipe for an incredibly negative – **and more hurtful** – world?

No wonder it's so easy to be negative. Each one of us feels that we've more or less got the right!

We've got to remind ourselves:

> Every one of us gets hurt.
> Getting hurt is "normal" in this world.
> We shouldn't be surprised when we get hurt.
> Getting hurt is not a sufficient reason to bitch and complain.

Ouch! Does that sound too negative? It's not meant to be. It's meant to be realistic. **Often our negative actions towards others are fuelled by an unrealistic assumption that we have the right to NOT be hurt.**

That will be a great world when that is true. In fact, the new creation will be like that. But right now, we're not quite there yet.

Sure – every one of us gets hurt, **but...**

Step 2: You can choose to come out bitter, or better

You don't get to choose whether hurtful things happen to you, but you do get to choose **how** you deal with them. And in every difficult situation, **you have a choice.** You can choose to come out **bitter**, or you can choose to come out **better**.

> *Hebrews 12:15*
> *See to it that no-one misses the grace of God and that no bitter root grows up to cause trouble and defile many.*

That's a very powerful picture of a "bitter root" growing up. It starts small – but eventually it can take over.

Imagine that someone has a beautiful, smooth front lawn – picture perfect. Clean and green! And yet, in this "perfect" lawn, one little root is allowed to develop. One little root of bitterness. Has this ever happened to your lawn? That little weed which you couldn't be bothered taking out, keeps growing and eventually takes over the whole lawn!

That's the way that bitterness can grow in us. It starts small – but if it is fed – if it is allowed to develop, then like the verse from Hebrews says it will *"cause trouble and defile many"*.

I've seen this happen in people as they get older. There are some folk who are just a teensy bit negative in their teens, but they become more negative and bitter as they grow older. If you let a negative heart keep growing, you end up as a bitter old person.

Have you ever noticed how people get "more so" as they get older? That is, the sweet, gentle 40 year old becomes "more so" in their old age, and ends up more sweet and more gentle. But the bitter or negative 40 year old also grows "more so" in their old age. They can end up more bitter and more negative.

You might have no choice as to whether you get hurt. But you always have a choice as to how you can respond to it. And no matter what's going on for you now; no matter what hurtful things people might say to you tomorrow; no matter how you get let down by a world that is stuffed up by sin; **you always have a choice as to how you respond to being hurt.**

You can choose to come out of difficult stuff **bitter**, or you can choose to come out **better**.

The person who is growing a negative heart will usually come out bitter. The person who is growing a positive heart will usually choose to come out better.

I don't know what hurtful things are going on for you at the moment. Things could be really bad. Things might be really unfair. You might be going through things that tear God's heart in two. But you need to understand something that is always true: **God wants to use whatever hurtful things are going on for you to strengthen you.**

"Whatever doesn't kill me only strengthens me."

It's like manure on your garden. You know – you want your plants to grow strongly – to be the best they can. So you carefully place all sorts of manure around the plant to fertilise it.

Now, imagine that you're the plant. How do you feel about having all this manure thrown at you? You might well complain. Manure is smelly, it's sticky, it's... well... it's not much fun at all! But you know what the manure will do for the plant.

It's never much fun when the world dumps lots of "poo" on you. And right now you might feel you're in the thick of it. And you probably feel that you have every right to complain. But remember this – being in the poo is never much fun – **but it does make excellent fertiliser!**

"You always have a choice as to how you respond to being hurt"

Sure – you've got to acknowledge the hurt. No use pretending that everything is fine and dandy when it's obviously not. But God wants to use whatever hurtful things are going on for you to strengthen you. You do have a choice to make.

If you want to grow a negative heart, decide that you will come out bitter. If you want to grow a positive heart, decide now that you will come out better.

Step 3: Negative words reflect a negative heart

"Come on! Lighten up! What's wrong with having some negative words? What's wrong with paying people back a bit? What's wrong with grumbling and complaining – I mean look at what I have to put up with? Can't I just say a few negative things from time to time?"

I understand what you mean. Sometimes I feel the same way. But here is the real problem with negative words. Listen to what Jesus says:

Matthew 12:34
"For out of the overflow of the heart the mouth speaks."

Remember the principle in Chapter 4? *"What's on the inside will always come out."*

Matthew 12:34 again
"For out of the overflow of the heart the mouth speaks."

Jesus is saying that the words that you speak are a dead give-away as to what your heart is really like. That's why your words matter. They show the true state of your heart.

> Negative words come from a negative heart.
> Put-down words come from a put-down heart.
> Complaining words come from a complaining heart.
> Hurtful words come from a hurtful heart.
> Dirty words come from a dirty heart.
> Angry words come from an angry heart.
> Bitter words come from a bitter heart.

Come on – God wants to do something brand new with your heart. He doesn't want that root of bitterness to grow. God wants to build in you a positive heart. God wants to build in you an encouraging heart. God wants to build in you a heart that will sow into other people's lives and inspire them to become the mighty men and women of God that is their destiny. With a positive heart, with an encouraging heart you can release people to achieve their God-given potential and build them up to be the men and women that God wants them to be.

How do I do that? Chapter 16!

16 three steps to a positve heart

How do I build a heart that is genuinely positive? How can I be that genuine encourager? How can I build others up without being insincere?

This can be a hard one. Overcoming negativity can be difficult in our culture. But God shows us the way. Here are 3 steps to grow a heart that is truly positive. 3 steps that will help you become "Awesome on the Inside".

Step 1: Build up, don't put down

There is a great verse in the Bible that shows us how to turn around our speech. It acts as a "filter" for everything that comes out of our mouth. If we could tape this scriptural filter across our mouths – you would see a whole new community of people who genuinely wanted to build others up.

Have you got your seat-belt fastened? Let's go!

> *Ephesians 4:29*
> *"Do not let any unwholesome talk come out of your mouths, but only what is helpful for building others up according to their needs, that it may benefit those who listen."*

There's a stack of stuff in that verse. Let's unpack the five key filters!

1. "... No unwholesome talk..."

God's plan for your mouth is that nothing "unwholesome" should come out of it. That gives us the first question you can ask of anything you're about to say:

> *"Is it wholesome?"*

Now "wholesome" and "unwholesome" aren't words that most of us use all the time. In fact "wholesome" sounds down-right boring. It's used to describe foods that allegedly have lots of nutrients, but actually taste like processed cardboard. "Wholesome" is one of those words used to describe those tacky U-rated family movies which might have nothing offensive in them, but also have nothing interesting in them either! No self-respecting teenager would ever buy a book called *"1000 Wholesome Jokes"*! *(Please don't take offence if you've just bought it!)*

But wholesome is a good word. It simply describes something that is "whole" or "complete". Wholesome words are simply those that are positive and complete. Words that build up – rather than words that tear down.

If you don't have food that is wholesome, you will end up unhealthy. If you don't have values that are wholesome, you will end up degraded. If you don't have a doctor who is wholesome, you will end up sick. If you don't have an accountant who is wholesome, you will end up broke! If you don't have words that are wholesome, you will end up negative and bitter.

> ## "Negative words come from a negative heart"

By putting the filter of no unwholesome talk over our mouths, a whole lot of unhelpful junk is immediately filtered out. God doesn't want us to have words which are negative, or a put-down, or angry, or insulting, or sarcastic, or complaining, or grumbling. Put quite simply, all that is unwholesome – it will never make you – or anyone else "whole".

That one piece of information might be enough for you to turn around your speech. However, if you need a little more help, here are some more great "positive" filters for your mouth.

2. "... Only what is helpful..."

There is the second question that you can ask of anything you say:

"Is it helpful?"

If what you are about to say will genuinely help the other person, then say it. If it won't help them, then **don't** say it!

3. "... For building others up..."

There is the third question that you can ask of anything you say:

"Will it build the other person up?"

If what you are about to say will genuinely build up the other person, then say it. If it won't build them up, then **don't** say it! Even if what you need to say is critical – because you're trying to instruct them or correct them – then check "Will the way I say this build them up or tear them down?"

4. "... According to their needs..."

There is the fourth question that you can ask of anything you say:

"Does the other person need to hear this?"

If the other person genuinely needs to hear what you have to say, then say it. If they don't need to hear it, then **don't** say it!

You might need to distinguish here between what you need to **say**, and what the other person needs to **hear**. Sometimes you will have a burning desire to say something to another person, but realistically, they don't need to hear it. I sometimes write a letter or email to another person – and get everything off my chest, **and then I never send it**. I needed to say it, but they didn't need to hear it. I have also had arguments with people "inside my head" where I say everything I need to say. But the other person might not need to hear all that detail. By the time I get to the other person, I can have a better chance of saying things that they genuinely need to hear.

5. "... That it may benefit those who listen..."

There is the fifth question that you can ask of anything you say:

"Will the other person benefit from hearing this?"

If the other person will genuinely benefit from hearing what you have to say, then say it. If they won't benefit from hearing it, then **don't** say it!

Imagine being part of a community where the only things we said to each other were to build each other up! Imagine having people genuinely wanting to strengthen each other by everything they said! Imagine being in a culture where even when someone had to be corrected, that it was done in a way that built them up.

*"But nobody else ever treats **me** this way?"*

Maybe not. But are you part of the problem, or part of the solution?

You have the power with the words you speak to cut down and tear away at people. And you have the power with the words you speak to build others up and to give life to everything they do.

As the Bible says:

> **Proverbs 18:21**
> *"The tongue has the power of life and death"*

There's the first step to building a positive heart – build up, don't put down.

Step 2: Look to the future, not the past

God's picture of you is always the person that you are becoming – not the person you are leaving behind. God is moulding you and shaping you and lining you up to be the person that he wants you to be. And it is this future focus which can keep God being incredibly positive about you.

Where you get negative – is where you look at things the way they used to be. *"I've always failed in this area. I'm just hopeless"*. Well maybe you once were – but God is moulding you to be different.

The way to build a positive heart is to stay focussed on where you are heading. That's what God does!

2 Corinthians 5:16-17

"So from now on we regard no-one from a worldly point of view. Though we once regarded Christ in this way, we do so no longer. Therefore, if anyone is in Christ, he is a new creation; the old has gone, the new has come!"

I'm not the person I used to be – but I'm still not the person I'm going to be! To grow a positive heart – you always focus on the person that someone will be in the future, rather than the person that they used to be in the past.

I've coached my son's football team for years. When they were very little, and didn't know that much about the beautiful game, how did I react when one of our full backs did a really awful kick that ended up going in our own goal?

I could have said *"You stupid idiot! That was the worst kick I have ever seen! You'll never be a great football player. For the sake of the team, I'm leaving you on the bench next week!"*

I have actually heard coaches say things like that. They failed all the "filter tests" of Ephesians 4:29. But they also focussed on the past – taking the poor kid back to all his mistakes.

I preferred to focus on the future. I would say something like this: *"One day you're going to be a great player. I want to help you get there. Can I show you some extra things at training which will help you become that great player?"*

If you want to build a positive heart in others, then focus on the possibilities that lie ahead of them – rather than taking them back to the mistakes of the past. You know this is right, because this is the way God treats you.

> I have worked with teenagers my whole life, and until recently, my own children were adolescents. You can never build up an adolescent by reminding them of their mistakes as a child!
> *"Well, I'm not sure that I can let you borrow the car. Remember – you pooed in your nappy when you were three!"*

"A positive heart will always focus on the future"

NO!!! The way you build anyone up is to focus on the future, rather than drag them back to the past. A negative heart will always focus on the past, and drag you back to wrong things that have already happened. That's the way Satan treats you.

A positive heart will always focus on the future, and inspire you onwards to good things that haven't yet come to pass. That's the way God treats you. So – are you going to ignore him – or join him?

Step 3: Learn to be an encourager.

To some people, this might come naturally. But to most of us, this is something we need to learn.

> *1 Thessalonians 5:11*
> *"Therefore encourage one another and build each other up, just as in fact you are doing."*

To encourage simply means to "give courage". Literally, it means to strengthen someone's heart. When you encourage someone, you give them the strength to help them unlock their potential.

I suspect that most of us know how to do this. You simply look for something good or something promising within a person – and you tell them about it in a way that spurs them on to do it more and more.

Why are we sometimes reluctant to do this? I suspect it goes something like this: *"I am feeling a little insecure myself. If I encourage and strengthen someone else, I might feel a little worse about myself. So I'll play it safe and not encourage them."*

I understand that feeling, but you know what? **It is rarely true!** I normally find that when I take the bold step to encourage someone else, that as well as "lifting them up", that **I too** am lifted up with them! Go on – try it – and check whether it's true!

"Go out and encourage someone!"

There is a character in the Bible called "Barnabus". *(You can read about him in Acts 4:33-37)*. His name literally means "Son of Encouragement". Wouldn't it be great to be known by that name! Imagine the difference you could make to people's lives if you were their constant encourager! Wouldn't it be fantastic if you were the person that helped release other people to fulfil their purpose and destiny!

You don't have to get it word perfect. It's okay if you get it wrong occasionally. But let's have a go! Who needs to hear a word of encouragement from you? Someone in your own family? (They need it every day!) Someone where you work? A friend at your school? Your pastor or leader at church? The bus driver? The person on the phone?

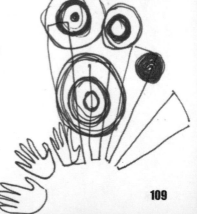

Go and speak works of life into someone. Send them a card or a note of appreciation. Fire off a positive email. Encourage them on the phone. Send them a text message. Go to it!

Try to imagine being part of a community where everyone is achieving their God-given potential because they are all champion encouragers who have learnt to grow positive hearts.

Well, go on! What are you waiting for?

Go out and encourage someone!

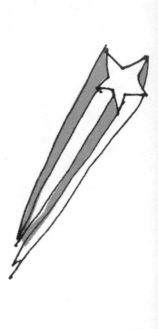

a heart that is pumping

section 6

"Awesome on the Inside" challenged me about whether I was really letting the Holy Spirit run my life, or whether I was just doing things in my own strength." **Tim, Year 10**

17 | stay where the action is

The excitement of being "up front"

It's the night of the big concert. Thousands of fans have packed into the auditorium. This is the night that everyone has been waiting for. The house lights go down... the stage lights go up... the smoke machine is pumping... and the band emerges on stage and belts out their music into the night.

Everyone has come to hear the band. Everyone is pumped. But there seem to be two classes of spectators at this big event. There are those sitting way-back in the stands – and there are those who are up-front on the dance floor.

Here's the question: Which group is more involved? Which group is more pumped? Which group is more passionate?

Imagine another picture. There are two groups of soldiers. The first group is on patrol in a war against terrorists. They have them pinned down in an abandoned village. The soldiers are in their trenches – rifles at the ready. They're not sure exactly where the terrorists are – but they know they're close. They realise they are on a life or death mission.

Back at Army headquarters, thousands of miles away, is another group of soldiers. They have retired from active duty. They support their colleagues, and they want to win the war. But they never actually **go** to war any more. They stay back at headquarters – they work from a desk, and enjoy swapping old stories with their army buddies as they sit around the bar.

Both groups are soldiers – both are committed to the same army – both want the same outcome in the war. But which group do you think is more passionate about the outcome? Which group is more committed? Which group do you think will stay more devoted and more faithful 24 hours a day?

Here is a lesson we can learn from the dance-floor and from the front-line trenches: if you want to be passionate, if you want to be committed, if you want to be enthusiastic and excited about what you're doing – then **stay where the action is!** It might be more **comfortable** to be way back in the stands, or back at Army headquarters, but it's the people in the front-lines who will remain the most passionate and devoted to their mission.

The passion of staying on the front-line

I remember when a youth minister from another church visited our youth ministry and observed how we ran things. Afterwards he was asking me questions about what he saw. One of his questions almost stumped me.

He asked:
"How do you keep your entrenched Christian students so enthusiastic and active?"

*"**Entrenched** Christian students?"* I asked

"Yeah – you know. They come from a Christian family, go to a Christian church, attend a Christian youth group and go to a Christian school. They play in a Christian sporting team, listen to Christian music, read Christian books and play Christian computer games. They live in a Christian home, play in their Christian backyard and go for walks with their Christian dog..."

I got the picture.

"We find these kids the hardest to reach. They're so uninvolved at our youth group, and they're always the first to criticise. But at your youth groups they're different. So – how do you keep your Christian teenagers so enthusiastic and active?"

I understood his question. And I agreed with his observation that our Christian students **were** enthusiastic and keen. But I have to admit, that on the spur of the moment, I could not think of anything we had **done** to produce that result.

And then it hit me. *"We simply keep them involved in front-line ministry"*

Front-line ministries are when you are out there on the cutting edge of Christianity. Front-line ministries are when you are directly standing for Jesus in the non-Christian world.

Front-line ministries include things like:

- Inviting your non-Christian friend at school to come to church.
- Volunteering at a homeless shelter.
- Talking about your faith with your friends on the footy team.
- Praying where people can see you at school.
- Helping your unchurched friend to become a Christian.
- Sitting with the kid who always has lunch by himself.
- Living in a Christlike way with your non-Christian parents.

Front-line ministries are when you are directly standing for Jesus in the non-Christian world.

Let me tell you five things about front-line ministries:

1. They will always stretch you.
2. You will never feel comfortable doing them.
3. They might be scary.
4. They are for every Christian (irrespective of your particular gifts).
5. They will keep you passionate and enthusiastic about your faith in Christ.

But most importantly – it's what God has called you to!

The dedication of a soldier

Let's look at one passage in the Bible where God calls us all to front-line ministries.

2 Timothy 2:3-4
Endure hardship with us like a good soldier of Christ Jesus. No-one serving as a soldier gets involved in civilian affairs – he wants to please his commanding officer.

When Paul wrote these words, he would have had a lot of time to observe the life of a soldier. He was in prison – in chains in some dungeon somewhere – being guarded by Rome's finest. He could have observed the absolute dedication that was required of anyone in the armed forces.

"If you want to stay passionate – stay where the action is!"

Note carefully what he says:

1. Endure hardship

A life of a soldier is not easy. You don't join the armed forces because you want a life of comfortable luxury. Being in the army is hard work. I don't think I'd even survive the first six weeksof basic training! Soldiers have to do all sorts of difficult things – go to war – and fight the enemy – and live in trenches – and eat meagre rations.

If you're going to be a good soldier, there's going to be hardship. The key to being a good soldier – is absolute dedication.

It's exactly the same with being a Christian. If you just become a Christian because of "all the great things I will get out of it – and how cool it will be for me" – you are on dangerous ground. Because when you sign up to be a Christian – you have enlisted for a battle. You are going out against an enemy – you're being sent to the front lines – and you'll be called upon by Jesus to do some things that will be really hard.

2. Don't get involved in civilian affairs

A soldier has to be totally focussed on what they're meant to achieve. It's not much use if some soldier – instead of carrying out orders – is off chasing their next date in the nearby village! If your commanding officer says "We're going to attack the next town tonight", you can't say back: *"Sorry – can't do that tonight. I've got a date with the girl next door"*

There are all sorts of things that will distract you from your ministry of standing up for Jesus. All sorts of "civilian affairs" that you can get involved with. You might end up doing things that have nothing to do with what God wants of you.

3. Please your commanding officer

Your aim as a soldier of Christ is to please your commanding officer. You want to have his values in your life. You want to support all his decisions. You want to obey his commands. You want to achieve the mission that he has planned for you.

And you know that Jesus' overall mission is to "make disciples of all nations" (Matthew 28:19). This is your front-line ministry – for life!

The trap to avoid

Here's the trap:
- It's easier to do training for evangelism than to actually evangelise.
- It's easier to write a document about feeding the starving than to actually feed the starving.
- It's easier to go on a discipleship camp, than to actually go and make disciples.
- It's easier to have a Bible study about helping the poor, than to actually help the poor.
- It's easier to learn a gospel outline, than to actually tell your friend about Jesus.

So here's something to check out. **Have you moved away from the trenches and gone back to the safety of the base?**

When Christians pull out of the front lines with their non-Christian friends – and retreat back into a holy huddle with all the other believers, nothing happens. God's kingdom is not extended. The devil is very happy. Because when you retreat into the comfort of continual Christian-land – **you lose your passion**.

Reading this book is a good thing. But this is not the front-line.
Going to church is good. But this is not the battlefield.
Reading your Bible, saying your prayers, going on a Christian camp – these are all good things, but the reason that all these things exist is so that you will be effective out there on the front-lines. God calls you into the fellowship of his people so that you will be equipped for battle out there.

What does it take to get you out there? Does it mean inviting your neighbour over for coffee? Does it mean you join the team that reaches out in your local schools? Does it mean you befriend the kids at school who are a long way from Jesus?

If you want to stay passionate – if you want to stay "cutting edge" – if you want to build your heart for ministry – if you want to grow to become "awesome on the inside" – then get back in the world

"Endure hardship like a good soldier of Christ Jesus"

– get back in the front-line – and have your passion renewed as you see the power of Jesus working through you to change lives.

Stay where the action is!

18 a spirit-filled heart

"I want to be a Christian, but sometimes it just seems too hard!"

Sound familiar? I bet you've said those same words yourself at some stage. You love Jesus – you want to live for him – but doing all the things that you've got to do to be a faithful Christian can sometimes just seem like **hard work!**

> Personally, I don't think I like working hard. If there's an easier way of doing things, I tend to look for it. When I was at school, my study and homework usually degenerated into a frantic last-minute rush to do the absolute bare minimum that would produce acceptable results! *(And some of my poor results prove that this is not a very good study method!)*

And sure – sometimes following Jesus **is** hard. There are some tough decisions to make; there's extra learning you've got to do; there are temptations you must fight; there are meetings to go to; commandments to obey; ministry jobs to be done...

But there's something good about being given to a high standard to aim for. Jesus does call us to be faithful soldiers in his army. There is something great about being used by God to change this world for him.

But it's not meant to be a burden! Jesus didn't call you to himself because he wanted to make your life **harder!** Jesus called you to follow him so he could make your life **better!**

Listen to the words of Jesus as he invites people to follow him:

> **Matthew 11:28-30**
> *"Come to me, all you who are weary and burdened, and I will give you rest. Take my yoke upon you and learn from me, for I am gentle and humble in heart, and you will find rest for your souls. For my yoke is easy and my burden is light."*

When Jesus calls people to follow him, he says *"I will give you rest... you will find rest for your souls."* He then talks about placing his "yoke" on us. The yoke he is talking about is the piece of timber that would be placed across the necks of two oxen so that they pulled together in their work on the farm. The "yoke" was the work – or the burden – that they were expected to achieve. When Jesus calls you to follow him, he gives you a yoke – that is, there is work that he wants you to achieve. But note carefully - he says *"my yoke is **easy** and my burden is **light**."*

"Jesus didn't call you to make your life harder. Jesus called you to make your life better!"

One of the traps of being a young enthusiastic Christian, is that you want to please Jesus more and more, and so you work harder and harder at it. You get challenged in an area of your life – so you work harder still. You want to be more faithful, so you put in extra effort. And you get to a point where it's so much hard work that you stop enjoying it.

Has this ever happened to you?

God has some great news for you! Sure – there is a high standard that God is calling to – but here's the good bit – **you don't have to do it in your own strength! God himself will give you the power to live the way he wants you to!**

That's right! Can you imagine having the power of God himself in your life – so that you can be the person that God really wants? Well, that's what God has done for every person who turns and follows his son Jesus. **He gives you his Holy Spirit so that you have the strength and power to live for him.**

Sit back and soak in what God wants you to know about his Holy Spirit. Enjoy the freedom of knowing that you don't have to do it all in your own strength. And let God unleash you as he grows within you a spirit-filled heart.

The Holy Spirit is God's gift

Whenever you say "yes" to Jesus – whenever you give your life to Christ – whenever you receive God's forgiveness and are adopted as his child into his family – God gives you the gift of his Holy Spirit. The Holy Spirit is God himself who lives within you – and if you have genuinely become a Christian, then God has already placed his Spirit in your life.

> **Romans 5:5**
> … *God has poured out his love into our hearts by the Holy Spirit, whom he has given us.*

If you have become a Christian, then you can know for certain that God has already placed his Holy Spirit in your life. In fact, you cannot belong to Christ unless you have God's Holy Spirit!

> **Romans 8:9**
> … *And if anyone does not have the Spirit of Christ, he does not belong to Christ.*

The Holy Spirit is God's power

Do you sometimes feel like you don't have the strength and power to live the way God wants? That maybe it's just too hard?

Well, think about this: When Jesus was dead in his tomb, how much power did it take to bring him back to life? How much energy did God need so that his tortured, crucified, dead and buried son would be brought back to life as the Lord of all creation?

> **"The Spirit who lives in you is the same Spirit who raised Jesus from the dead!"**

How much power did it take? A couple of AA alkaline batteries? 240 volts from a power point? 100,000 volts from an electricity substation? Come on – it would have been far more than this! This is the ultimate miracle! A man who is dead and buried is brought back to life as the conqueror of the universe! This would have taken all the powers of heaven to produce such a magnificent transformation!

Guess what? **That same power is now unleashed in your life so that you will also be transformed!**

Check this out!

Romans 8:11
"And if the Spirit of him who raised Jesus from the dead is living in you, he who raised Christ from the dead will also give life to your mortal bodies through his Spirit, who lives in you."

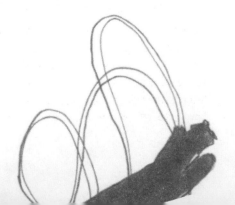

God's word tells us that the Spirit who now lives in you **is the same Spirit who raised Jesus from the dead!** So – how much power is now available to you so that you can be transformed to be the person that God really wants? **Exactly the same!** Are you getting a sense of how exciting it is to have the Holy Spirit living in your life? The Spirit is God's power to change you to be the way he wants. You don't have to do it all under your own strength!

The Holy Spirit is God's guarantee

How do you know that you genuinely belong to God? And how do you know that you will receive all the things that God has promised you? Simple! God has given you his Holy Spirit who guarantees both things!

> *Ephesians 1:13-14*
> *And you also were included in Christ when you heard the word of truth, the gospel of your salvation. Having believed, you were marked in him with a seal, the promised Holy Spirit, who is a deposit guaranteeing our inheritance until the redemption of those who are God's possession – to the praise of his glory.*

1. The guarantee that you belong to God

In the above passage from Ephesians 1, people who truly believe in Jesus are described as being *"marked in him with a seal, the promised Holy Spirit"*. What does this mean?

> # "The Holy Spirit is God's guarantee that you belong to him"

In ancient days, if you were writing someone a letter, you didn't get to put it in an envelope. You would roll it up and drip some melted wax over the join – and as the wax hardened, that would seal your letter up until it was time for it to be opened. If the letter came from someone important – like the king – he would have a "seal" – a metal imprint with his crest on it – and before the wax became hard, he would press his "seal" into the wax, so that when it hardened, it had a permanent imprint in it. Anyone who received the letter would then know that it came with the authority of the king. It was the stamp of ownership by the king.

The Bible tells us that when we believe in God, he puts his stamp of ownership on us – he "seals" us with his Holy Spirit to guarantee that we belong to him. It's like his trademark – or a branding iron on cattle. If you are a Christian, God has "branded" you to say: "This person belongs to me". The fact that God has given you his Holy Spirit is his guarantee that you really belong to him.

2. The guarantee that you will receive God's promises

In the above passage from Ephesians 1, the Holy Spirit is described as being *"a deposit guaranteeing our inheritance"*. What does this mean?

This means that the Holy Spirit is the "first payment" by God that guarantees that you will receive every other payment that he has promised. The Spirit *"guarantees our inheritance"*.

Imagine you are buying a car for £10,000. You sit in the office of the car dealer. There are papers to be signed, forms to be completed. Now comes the time when you hand over your money to take possession of your car. You pass £10,000 across to the dealer – and what does he give you back? A little piece of paper – and a little bit of metal! The little piece of paper is the registration document to your new car –and the little bit of metal is the key that unlocks your car.

You might think to yourself *"I've just handed over £10,000 – and all I got back was a little bit of paper and a tiny lump of metal!"* But you know that they are your guarantees. The little bit of paper guarantees that that car belongs to you. And that little bit of metal means you get to drive whatever it unlocks.

God's Holy Spirit is just like that. He is like the "key" that God gives you that guarantees that you get everything! God's Holy Spirit will unlock every one of God's promises! God wants to bless you abundantly throughout eternity

– and the gift of his Holy Spirit is his first gift to you – which guarantees you that you will receive **everything else** that God has promised! How cool is that?

> ## "God's Holy Spirit will unlock every one of God's promises"

The Holy Spirit changes you

You understand the picture of what you used to be like – sinful, disobedient, ignoring God and living as his enemy. You understand the picture of what God wants you to be – Christ-like, obedient, worshipping God and living as his faithful servant.

You've made the change to follow Christ. But how do you **keep** making the change to become **more** like Christ? You've said to God "I will obey you." But how do you keep turning from your sin so that you are **actually** obeying him more and more every day? How do you become less and less like your old sinful self – and more and more like your new Christ-controlled self?

Great news! **That's what the Holy Spirit does!** He will keep working in your life to make you more and more like Jesus!

> ### 2 Corinthians 3:17-18
> ... *And we, who with unveiled faces all reflect the Lord's glory,*
> *are being transformed into his likeness with ever-increasing glory,*
> *which comes from the Lord, who is the Spirit.*

Did you catch what God's Spirit is doing for you?

1. You are being transformed!

The passage from 2 Corinthians says you *"are being transformed into his likeness"*. That is - you are being transformed into the likeness of Jesus himself! God's Spirit is at work in your life to make you less like your old sinful self, and more like your new Christ-controlled self!

This is great stuff! But wait... there's more!

2. You are being transformed more and more!

The passage from 2 Corinthians says you *"are being transformed into his likeness **with ever-increasing glory"***.

That's right! God's Holy Spirit will keep changing you more and more – so that you will become just like Jesus – even more – every day!

How brilliant is that!

- God's Holy Spirit wants to change your **obedience** to become more and more like Jesus.
- God's Holy Spirit wants to change your **values** to become more and more like Jesus.
- God's Holy Spirit wants to change your **character** to become more and more like Jesus.
- God's Holy Spirit wants to change your **prayer-life** to become more and more like Jesus.

Sure – you need to make some crucial decisions. You need to make the hard calls. You need to actively turn away from sins that you know will drag you down. You need to remain immersed in God's word and surround yourself with the fellowship of God's people. **But you don't have to struggle on your own!** God has given you his Holy Spirit to keep changing you to be more and more like Jesus himself!

The Holy Spirit equips you for ministry

We saw in the last chapter that there is a job that God wants you to do. There is a world that needs to be brought into subjection to his son. You have friends who need to hear about Jesus. Jesus has called you to his ministry team, and given you a part in changing this world.

But how do I do that?

The Holy Spirit will equip you for ministry! Here are two ways that happens:

1. God's Spirit gives you ministry gifts

> *1 Corinthians 12:4-7*
> *There are different kinds of gifts, but the same Spirit. There are different kinds of service, but the same Lord. There are different kinds of working, but the same God works all of them in all men. Now to each one the manifestation of the Spirit is given for the common good.*

Here's a quick translation of those verses! *"God's Spirit gives different ministry gifts to different people – but they all come from the same God. Each Christian is given some ministry gifts for the benefit of others."*

That means that, if you are a Christian, and God's Spirit has been given to you, then you have already received a "gift" or "ability" to minister to others. It might take you a while to work out what you're really good at in ministry – and you might need your fellow Christians around you to give you some guidance on this. But here is something that you can know for sure – **if you are a Christian, God's Spirit has already equipped you for ministry!** You don't just have to go out and do it all by yourself!

2. God's Spirit helps you when you need it

As you read the Bible, you will see that God's Spirit guides his people when they need his help. This can happen in all sorts of ways. You know you will hear God's voice as you read the Bible – but God can also guide you in any way he wants.

Listen to a promise that Jesus gave to his immediate disciples:

Matthew 10:19-20

But when they arrest you, do not worry about what to say or how to say it. At that time you will be given what to say, for it will not be you speaking, but the Spirit of your Father speaking through you.

What Jesus is saying here is that when you are put on the spot – when you're in a situation where you need to say something about Jesus, but

"God's Holy Spirit will keep making you more and more like Jesus"

you're not quite sure what to say, you can trust God's Holy Spirit to guide you – and to speak through you. You are not by yourself! The Spirit of your Father will speak through you.

This is just the greatest news that you need as a Christian! You don't have to battle on by yourself. You don't have to do it in your own strength. God is not expecting you to just work harder and harder and harder until you collapse under the weight of trying to live for Jesus.

God has already given you his Holy Spirit. He has already given you the strength and power that you need to live for him. His own Holy Spirit has been given to you – to live in you – to change you – and equip you.

But how do you tap into the power of this Holy Spirit? How do you make sure that you are trusting in his strength – and not in your own?

Read on!

19 how to tap into god's power

So, if God's Spirit is making all this power available – how do I make it happen in my life? What does God's word tell me to do so that I am trusting in God's strength, rather than my own?

Here are five steps from the New Testament:

Step 1: Keep being filled with God's Spirit

There is an interesting verse in Ephesians:

> *Ephesians 5:18*
> *Do not get drunk on wine, which leads to debauchery.*
> *Instead, be filled with the Spirit.*

Now there's a whole lot of good info in the Bible about not getting drunk. *(We'll get into that another time!)* But notice here what the **alternative** is – *"instead, be filled with the Spirit."*

> *Hang on – if I've already received God's Spirit when I became a Christian, why do I still need to be 'filled'?*

That's a good question. In one sense, you don't need any "more" of the Spirit, because you received the **whole** of the Holy Spirit when you gave your life to Jesus! It's not like God has only given you a half-measure, and you need to face up to him again and plead "Can I have some more?"

And it's not like you need "topping up" with the Spirit because somehow you've lost a bit. You know, a little bit has trickled out here, and little bit more has leaked over there.

When the Bible urges us to "be filled with the Spirit", it's not talking about being "filled up because we're a little bit empty". Being "filled" with the Spirit really means being "controlled" by God's Spirit, or being "consumed" by God's Spirit.

Have you ever heard of someone who was "filled with anger"? It doesn't mean that they were a little bit empty of anger and were being topped up! It means they were "controlled" by their anger – or "consumed" by their anger.

So God wants us to keep being open to being controlled by his Spirit. **That's** why it's the alternative to getting *"drunk on wine"*. It's a question of what will control you. God is saying *"Don't let alcohol (or anything else) control you. Let my Spirit control you."*

> ## "Being 'filled' with God's Spirit means being 'controlled' by God's Spirit"

So the first way to tap into the Spirit's power, is to keep being open to having God's Spirit control you. Get stuck into reading God's word. Get stuck into prayer. And ask God's Holy Spirit to keep taking charge of your life – so you live by the Spirit rather than by your own thoughts and actions.

You can read more about being led by God's Spirit in **Romans 8: 5-14.**

Step 2: Keep in step with God's Spirit

Galatians 5:25
Since we live by the Spirit, let us keep in step with the Spirit.

You know what it means to "keep in step" with someone else?

There is an army marching on parade. All the soldiers are united together as one unit. They wear the same uniform. They travel in the same direction. **And they keep in step with each other.** "Keeping in step" simply means that they do **exactly** the same as each other.

Or... there's a group of dancers on the stage. There is one lead

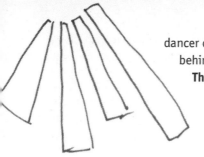

dancer out the front. There is a chorus line behind her, and they follow her every move. **They keep in step with her.**

Imagine how it would look if one soldier on parade was out of step with everyone else! Imagine how the dancers would look if one person couldn't keep in step with the others!

In the same way, God wants you keep in step with his Spirit. God's Spirit has a path that he wants you to walk down. God's Spirit sets the lead and expects you to follow. Keeping in step means you follow exactly what your leader says. Imagine being in a group of Christians, where you are the only one who is "out of step"!

"God himself will give you the power to live the way he wants to"

Where is God leading you? What steps does he want you to follow? Is there an area of your life where you are "out of step" with God?

Step 3: Don't resist God's Spirit

Acts 7:51
You stiff-necked people, with uncircumcised hearts and ears! You are just like your fathers: You always resist the Holy Spirit!

God uses his Holy Spirit to prompt you to obey. You might be reading something in God's word. It might even be a passage that you have read many times before. But you suddenly become aware of something in the verse that God is focusing you on. You know that these are not just printed words. God has something to say to you! This is the work of the Holy Spirit. He takes the message of God's word and applies it to your heart. When you know that God's Holy Spirit is speaking to you – **don't resist him!**

Can you think of times in your life where God's Spirit has been calling you to a new area of obedience, and you have resisted? Are there some issues that you need to fix up with God right now?

Step 4: Don't grieve the Holy Spirit

Ephesians 4:30
And do not grieve the Holy Spirit of God, with whom you were sealed for the day of redemption.

If you read all the verses that surround this one, you will see they all have to do with personal obedience. The way you "grieve" the Holy Spirit is to continue to defy what he is clearly teaching you. Look at some of the instructions that surround this verse:

> *"put off falsehood"*
> *"speak truthfully"*
> *"in your anger do not sin"*
> *"do not give the devil a foothold"*
> *"he who has been stealing must steal no longer"*
> *"do not let any unwholesome talk come out of your mouths"*
> *"get rid of all bitterness, rage and anger, brawling and slander, along with every form of malice"*
> *"be kind and compassionate to one another, forgiving each other"*

Right in the middle of that list of instructions, God says, *"do not grieve the Holy Spirit of God"*. Wouldn't it be terrible if in your personal life – those deep-down sins that you keep hoping no-one will notice – wouldn't it be terrible if you were actually grieving the Spirit of God?

Step 5: Don't put out the Spirit's fire

1 Thessalonians 5:19-21
"Do not put out the Spirit's fire; do not treat prophecies with contempt. Test everything..."

It's interesting that in the Scriptures, the work of God's Spirit is described like a "fire". **Equally** interesting is that we are warned not to put the fire out!

How might we put out the Spirit's fire? The next sentence gives us an example: *"Do not treat prophecies with contempt"*. While the New Testament never precisely defines what prophecy is – it certainly has to do with taking God's word and applying it to the life of an individual. It is a good example of a ministry that is guided by God's spirit.

So – don't put out the Spirit's fire by treating his work with contempt! Now I know we want to be careful to get things right. We want to make sure that Christians aren't **abusing** the work of God's Holy Spirit. But let's not be over-critical! Just because someone is being led by God's Spirit in a way that we don't fully understand, doesn't necessarily mean it's wrong. As long as it fits in with what God has already told us in his word – rejoice that someone else is being blessed by it! Don't treat the work of the Spirit with contempt!

"Don't put out the Spirit's fire"

But there is a warning at the end of that verse. It simply says *"test everything"*. Not everything that looks like it is coming from God's Spirit might actually **be** from God's Spirit. So test it! Test it against what the scriptures say. Test whether it fits in with God's revealed character. Check out whether other Christians understand it the same way.

In our staffroom at work, there is a fridge. Lots of people store things in that fridge. And sometimes, they forget to clear them out. Some of the things in our staff fridge can end up **very old and out-of-date**.

Whenever I use something from that fridge, I test it first. If I'm pouring a glass of milk, when I remove the container from the fridge, I open it and pass it under my nose to "sniff" it. I want to know whether it will be good for me, or not! I test everything!

In the same way, "test" everything that looks like it comes from the Spirit. If someone tells you something, and says it is from God, then test it! Confirm it with another trusted Christian before you act on it. If people believe that God has told them something, test it against what he has already said in the Bible – because you know God will never contradict himself. If you come up with an idea – and you think it's from God's Spirit – test it against what other Christians understand on the same subject.

But don't treat the Spirit's work with contempt! Don't put out the fire of the Holy Spirit! Tap into the power that God has provided and live a life that is led by God's Spirit. Then you will grow to be Awesome on the Inside!

20 a brand new heart

Right now, you're probably having one of two thoughts.

Here's the first possibility: You've read through the book – you've checked out the Bible – you've spoken to God in prayer – and you know that by the mighty work of the Holy Spirit, God is rebuilding you from the inside out. Your prayer life is deepening, you are growing in your passion to follow Jesus, you're asking God to help you have a heart that is pure, and you are being a genuine encourager to people around you. It's not always easy – but you know you are growing!

Is that you? Well done! You probably don't need this chapter! You can skip straight to Chapter 21!

On the other hand, you might be thinking to yourself *"I still don't get it! I've tried everything, but nothing has changed! I don't feel 'Awesome on the Inside' one little bit! What did I miss?"*

Maybe you can tick all the boxes, but you don't feel that there's any difference. You say your prayers, you read your Bible, you mix with other Christians (or maybe you don't even do that!) – but you sense there's really nothing different inside at all. Okay – there's something else that I need to alert you to. There is something else that you **might** have missed. If you're feeling that you've missed something vital on this journey, then this chapter is for you!

Our problem

I heard about a bloke who had a stray cat show up in his garage. It had no ID tag. He asked around – it appeared to have no owner. He didn't really know anything about cats – but he kept it.

He immediately struck problems. It wouldn't eat. It wouldn't drink its milk. He bought it a flea collar. He bought it a little basket to sleep in. But it wouldn't come inside. He brushed its fur. He gave it toys. But he got nothing. No response at all. Nothing!

After a week or so, a strange smell came from the garage. He discovered why his little cat wouldn't do anything. The whole time – **it had been dead!** That's why it wouldn't eat! That's why it wouldn't drink! That's why it wouldn't respond to him with any affection whatsoever.

He could do everything he liked. But if it was dead – nothing would work!

In the same way, you might be genuinely trying to do all the things that a Christian should do. Praying, reading the Bible, being "good"... but deep down you know there's something missing.

"If you're dead on the inside – nothing will work"

Maybe we can learn a lesson from that dead cat. No matter how good you are on the outside – no matter how many good and Christian things you do, if you're still dead on the inside – nothing will work.

Dead on the inside? What do you mean?

Here it is as simply as I can put it. To be alive as a Christian, you need God to give you a new heart.

If deep down you know that you've never really taken the step of saying "yes" to Jesus – and you know that you've never handed your life over to his control – then maybe this is the one step that you've missed on this whole journey.

Let's quickly check out how God can bring you from "death" to "life" – and give you a new heart that is on fire for him. Here are some of God's great promises from **Ezekiel 36:25-28**:

God's Promises

1. God will cleanse you

> *Ezekiel 36:25*
> *I will sprinkle clean water on you, and you will be clean;*
> *I will cleanse you from all your impurities and from all your idols.*

All of us have a problem with sin. We all do stuff that we know is wrong. This is the stuff that makes us "impure". This is the stuff that stains our relationship with Jesus. We might be great people in our own right, but the dirtiness of our sin weighs down on us and stops us having the relationship with God that we desperately want.

Here is God's great promise. Whatever sin there is in you, God says *"I will make you clean!"*

2. God will give you a new heart

> *Ezekiel 36:26*
> *I will give you a new heart and put a new spirit in you; I will*
> *remove from you your heart of stone and give you a heart of flesh.*

God promises that when you turn to his son Jesus, he will take out your old, rebellious heart and give you a brand new heart. God is not just offering to fix you up "on the outside". He is promising to make things new "on the inside". That's what God offers to people who truly turn to him. He offers them a brand new life.

3. God's Spirit will enable you to follow him

> *Ezekiel 36:27*
> *And I will put my Spirit in you and move you to follow my decrees*
> *and be careful to keep my laws.*

God doesn't just call you to follow him, and then leave you

simply to your own devices. It's not just up to us to try and manufacture the human strength to stick with him. No – God himself promises that he will place his Spirit in us so that we will have his strength available to follow his decrees and keep his laws. God promises his Holy Spirit to all those who are prepared to turn and follow his Son.

"God wants to give you a new heart"

4. God will take you to be with him forever

> *Ezekiel 36:28*
> *You will live in the land I gave your forefathers; you will be my people, and I will be your God.*

Of course, when God's Old Testament people first heard this, they would have only thought about the ancient geographical land of Israel that God had promised to their ancestors. But we know that that was really a symbol of the eternal land that God will give his people where they can enjoy him forever. God is planning a whole new creation where every one of his enemies is defeated – and where he will rule the universe in perfection forever. And here's the good news – **he wants you to be part of it!**

That's what God means when he says he wants to give you a new heart. Maybe this is the step that he is calling on you to take right now!

But how do I take that step?

This is where you need some other Christians around you to care for

you and guide you. Link up with them now, because they are part of a community that God has designed to grow you and nurture you and help you become the person that he wants you to be. You are joining a "forever" community. Don't take this step alone!

What Jesus has done

Jesus has done everything that needs to be done so that you can spend your eternity with God. Any sin – any barrier – that might have stopped you from getting to heaven – has already been dealt with by Jesus. Here's what he has already accomplished:

1. He committed no sin

> *1 Peter 2:22*
> *He committed no sin, and no deceit was found in his mouth.*

Jesus is the perfect Son of God. When he came and lived among us as a man, he always chose to obey his heavenly Father. He never sinned. This makes him uniquely qualified to deal with our sins.

2. He took our sins

> *1 Peter 2:24*
> *He himself bore our sins in his body on the tree, so that we might die to sins and live for righteousness; by his wounds you have been healed.*

When Jesus died on the cross, he took the sins of all those who would turn and follow him – and he placed them on himself. There on the cross he suffered for our sins; there on the cross he took God's punishment for our sins; there on the cross he offers us complete forgiveness from every sin. And when he rose from the dead three days later, he showed he has the power to give eternal life to anyone who comes to him.

3. He brought us back to God

1 Peter 2:25
For you were like sheep going astray, but now you have returned to the Shepherd and Overseer of your souls.

By his death and resurrection, Jesus has brought us back from going away from God, and has returned us into his loving arms. Everything that needed to be done so that God could make you his child has already been done. Everything that needed to be done so that God would give you a new heart, has already been done. Jesus has done everything that was required. Now he is waiting for you.

4. What you need to do

If you've never said "yes" to Jesus – if you know you want to accept what Jesus has done for you – if you're ready to take the step of handing your whole life over to Jesus, then all you have to do is ask.

Romans 10:9
... if you confess with your mouth, "Jesus is Lord," and believe in your heart that God raised him from the dead, you will be saved.

A: Check that you're ready

You do need to check that you are ready to start treating Jesus as Lord. That means that when you give your life to him – you mean it. That means that you will have a whole lifetime ahead of you learning to live the new life that he has created for you. There will be things that you know you will need to start doing. There might be things that you know you need to stop doing. But God promises that when you're ready to submit to Jesus

"If you've never taken the step of handing your life to Jesus – all you have to do is ask"

as your Lord, and you trust that in his death and resurrection he has done everything that you need to come back to God, then **you will be saved**.

Look again at the verse from Romans just above. The promise from God is certain. All you have to do is ask.

B: Ask God to change you

You can do it right now. Talk to God in your own words. Tell him that you have sinned and that you don't deserve his friendship. Tell him that you are placing all your trust in Jesus' death and resurrection that you might be forgiven. Ask him to take away every one of your sins; ask him to take your life over and start running it his way; ask him to give you a brand new heart so that you can serve him for the rest of eternity. Commit your life into his hands.

Are you ready? Use your own words. You can do it right now!

C: Join God's forever community

God never planned for you to have to fly solo. No-one is meant to struggle all by themselves. He has created a community of people where you can learn and grow. If you already belong to a church, then talk this through with someone you trust. If you don't yet belong to a church, catch up with one of your friends who does, and ask them to invite you.

Welcome to your new life! You have a lifetime of learning and growing ahead of you! And God has promised that he will be with you every step of the way!

God wants you to be "awesome on the inside". My prayer is that this book has helped you start the most exciting adventure of your life!

"I don't have to 'give up' on growing a godly character, because God's Spirit – who had the power to raise Jesus from the dead – is living in me!" **Ingrid, Year 12**

21 a new beginning

God wants to build you to be "awesome on the inside". He wants to build your heart.

> He wants you to grow a **powerful** heart.
> He wants you to grow a **prayerful** heart.
> He wants you to grow a **passionate** heart.
> He wants you to grow a **pure** heart.
> He wants you to grow a **positive** heart.
> He wants you to grow a **"pumping"** heart – Spirit-filled and ready for action!

Where are you being challenged? What does God want you to do differently? Starting today, what changes is God's Holy Spirit prompting you to take? Don't keep it all to yourself – if you are serious about growing to be "awesome on the inside", then share your thoughts with some trusted Christians so that we can all help each other to grow.

God has an awesome plan for you. God has a destiny that he wants you to achieve. God has given you the privilege of being on his team – and you get the joy of helping to bring this world to follow him – one life at a time.

May this be the start of a whole new chapter in your life, where God really does grow you to be **"awesome on the inside"**!

"God wants you to grow to be Awesome on the Inside"

Acknowledgements

Thanks heaps...

★ **To Jesus Christ.** Without you, not only would there be no book, but I would have no life. You have taken me to The Father, and filled me with your Spirit. Without you, I can do nothing.

★ **To my wife, Karen.** Without you, I could not do this ministry. I deeply appreciate the way you put up with me as I wrote each page. You've made lots of helpful comments and timely corrections to what I have written. I love you!

★ **To my daughter Carly, and my son Joshua.** The youth ministry "out there" means nothing to me compared with the joy of bringing you two through to Christian adulthood. Thanks for putting up with me as your dad.

★ **To Tim van Rees and Luke Davie.** Thank you for the brilliant cover design, and for all the great artwork throughout the book.

★ **To my sister, Karen Hawkins** for doing the final proof-reading and editing. You are a legend!

★ **To some very special students who helped me finish this book:** A number of students from Crossfire took the time to read through my manuscript – and come back to me with all sorts of helpful suggestions. This book is so much better because of you! So thank you to: *Gilbert Corr, Victoria Thwaites, Melissa Whale, Ryan Perryman, Tim Price, Lisa Pollard, Michael Harris, Tim Hooton, Ingrid van Woerkom and Alicia Bearman.*

To the many gifted Bible teachers who have sown into my life over the decades: I have been blessed over the decades by being taught God's word faithfully by a myriad of people – many of you would barely know that I exist. Thanks especially to **Dewey Bertolini** for teaching me so much about integrity, and to **Brian Houston** who first opened my eyes to the Bible's teaching on negativity.

To the students and leaders at *Crossfire* in sunny downtown Castle Hill. Thank you for allowing me to take you on the exciting journey of having your life turned around by Jesus. I love hanging out with you guys and I know God will use you to impact this world.

I have taken great care to give due credit to the number of individuals who have impacted my life and ministry. After almost three decades in ministry, it is possible that I have inadvertently included material which has not been properly acknowledged. If this has happened, please contact the publisher so that this can be rectified in future editions.